The legacy of a love

Marco Mohican

First printed edition: June 2021

marcomohican@gmail.com

ISBN 979-12-200-6737-9

9 791220 067379

Beautiful Isabel
I thank you for all the wonderful emotions you made me feel and all the lessons that you imparted me.
I entrust my version of our story to you,
hoping you will read and reflect on it.
Sincerely yours
Elias

A new start

When my marriage in Australia ended, I moved to New Zealand and eventually found a job as a public bus driver in Queenstown, a tourist mecca in the South Island. About six months later I met Meili, a very beautiful and multimillionaire Chinese woman who always took my bus and sat in the first row for a couple of rounds in the city, just to be with me. Meili showed an unprecedented interest in me and brought me gifts, so despite her inadequate English, we soon became a couple.

One day she asked me:

«Would you like to come with me for a trip to China?»

«Yes of course, I have never been there.»

«I will show you the best of my country for three months and pay all expenses.»

«Really, for three months?»

«Yes!»

«But why?»

«Because you are funny and I like you.»

«Well thank you. It would be very generous of you.»

A few days later she went to China while I kept wondering about her incredible offer and therefore consulted my colleagues and friends who knew about us:
«Guys, I can't believe it, it's too good to be true.»
«Don't think about it, just do it.»
«But how is it possible that such a beautiful and rich woman chooses me, a poor bus driver?»
«Elias, you have been lucky, but don't try to analyze it.
Go with her to China and enjoy yourself.»
«Yes, but I hope it's not going to become a disappointment.»

When she returned to New Zealand, she introduced me to Lian, her 24-year-old daughter who also lived in Queenstown. Then she asked me to go and live with her and after I had moved in her house, she started to talk about marriage:
«I want us to get married soon.»
«You can have any other man you desire.»
«I want you!»
«You flatter me, but what is the hurry?
We have known each other only for two months.»
«Do you really love me?»
«Yes of course.»
«Then why wait?»
«Well, to get to know each other better.»
«I think we know each other well enough by now. My friend and her New Zealander husband got married here just one week after they met and now two years later, they are still happy together.»
«Wow, that's quick. Okay, let me think about it for a while.»

Everything seemed surreal like a miracle, so after having asked her father's blessing in China, I secretly organized the proposal. One evening after dinner in the restaurant of a wheeled steamer on Lake *Wakatipu*, I surprised her and kneeling on deck in front of her, I presented her with an engagement ring:

«Beautiful Meili

it has been a great pleasure meeting you ever since the first time you boarded my bus and in every other occasion in which you came to see me with a gift.

It wasn't difficult to fall in love with a wonderful woman like you, who has made me wishing to have you by my side forever.

I love you with all my heart. Will you marry me?»

«Yes!»

Then I put on her finger a nice white gold ring with a one carat diamond of excellent quality which was only about half the size of that huge precious stone she usually wore. We kissed and then celebrated with dessert and a bottle of Moët.

Shortly after the engagement she told me:

«I want us to get married in a luxurious hotel in my hometown Chongqing, where I want to invite a thousand guests.»

«A thousand guests? Do you really know that many people?»

«Yes, I have a very big family and many friends all over China. Later on I will introduce you to my ex-tv producer colleagues.»

«Why?»

«Because you have a talent to become a comedian.»

«Me? A comedian, and in China?»

«Yes, as I told you before, you are very funny.»

«Do you really believe in me?»
«Absolutely, if you can manage to make people laugh the way you make me, you could have a huge success in China.»
«What a wonderful idea, okay I will try it.»

I told my family about this wonderful woman who not only had offered me love, but also an excellent opportunity for fame and fortune. Everything was going well and her English was slowly improving when one day she asked me:
«Are you marrying me for money?»
«No, what kind of question is this?»
«I have to know if you really love me.»
«Yes, I truly love you for the woman you are and not for your wealth. Why do you think like that?»
«Because my last husband forced me to pay him five million dollars before accepting to divorce.»
«Damn!»
«If you are not marrying me for money, will you give me a prenuptial agreement?»
«It's you who want us to get married.»
«Yes, but how would I know your true intentions?»
«I understand your concern and as I said before, we still don't know each other well enough.
You want a prenup for your peace of mind?
Fine, I will gladly sign you one.»
«Great, I will ask my lawyer to draft it.»
«Okay, but make sure that the prenup covers the interests of both of us.»

One day I called my ex-wife in Sydney:
«Hi Sara, how are you?»
«Hi Elias, I am fine. How is life in Queenstown?»
«It's alright and I have good news. I have met a beautiful and rich Chinese woman who wants to marry me.»
«How wonderful, you are so lucky.»
«I don't know why she is interested in me when she can have a rich man.»
«Don't think about it, it's her choice. What is her name?»
«Her name is Meili, she is forty-eight and she is an ex-dancer and tv producer.»
«Cool! I am very happy for you.
I too have some news that I would like to share with you.»
«Yeah, what is it?»
«I've been living with a man for a while, but I didn't want to tell you before for fear of upsetting you.»
«No, it's great; you know I have always wanted your happiness. Tell me more about him.»
«His name is David and he works where I work, but he guides tourists in the hinterland of Royal National Park.»
«Does he love you?»
«I think so.»
«Excellent! How is the family?»
«They are well and greet you.»
«I am happy for you and wish you all the best.»
«And I wish happiness for you and Meili.»
«Thanks, we talk again.»
«Yes sure, bye Elias.»

I didn't like my job, it was too stressful and I didn't make enough to satisfy Meili's expectations, so one day she asked me:
«Why don't you do something else?»
«I have tried to find a better job, but there is nothing else.»
«What do you think about a business?»
«Yes, I would like to become a chocolatier, but my capital has been frozen in Swedish kronor for some time.»
«How come?»
«A while ago I bought a bank draft to return to Sweden, but then I decided to stay. So if I change it back to dollars now, I would lose a lot of money in unfavorable exchange rate.»
«Why don't you quit your job anyway?»
«And then what would I do to earn a living?»
«I can finance what is necessary for you to set up a business of your choice.»
«What? Are you kidding me?»
«No, I am very serious, I promise you.»
«That would be great, but why?»
«Because I love you and I want you to be happy.»
«How sweet of you. Okay, I promise to reimburse you as soon as I can access my capital.»
«No, you don't have to repay me.»
«Thanks, but it wouldn't be my business if you finance it.»
«Elias, what do you say if we get married here in Queenstown and later on we organize the wedding reception in Chongqing?»
«I really don't care where we get married, as long as we go to China later on.»
«Yes of course, we will do it anyway.»

I resigned from my job and a few days later we got married in the city hall without even exchanging any wedding rings in the presence of Lian and a couple of my friends as witnesses. After about a month she told me it was time to go to China to meet her family and for our honey moon around the country. About a week later we went to Shanghai where a scruffy chain-smoking driver in a mediocre limousine drove us to a nice five-star hotel, courtesy of one of Meili's friends. When we went out the next day, she left me in the limousine in some street for about half an hour to go and meet someone and when I tried to find out who she had seen, she refused to tell me. In the evening we met one of her lady friends for dinner in a very posh restaurant. She spoke an excellent English, but I never thought replying to her questions would make Meili feel uncomfortable.
That night in the hotel room she asked me:
«What do you think about my friend?»
«She seems like a wonderful lady.»
«Do you think she is beautiful?»
«Yes, but not as much as you.»
«Do you fancy her?»
«What are you getting at?»
«Would you like to go out with her?»
«What? No, why would I want to date her?»
«Then why did you kiss her hand when saying good bye?»
«I did it as a common courtesy, just like when I bow to people to show them respect.»
«I don't like it and you must stop doing it.»
«Okay.»

«The next time we meet any of my friends, I want you to have a constant physical contact with me.»
«What do you mean?»
«You must hold my hand or touch my leg with yours so others can see your affection for me.»
«Really?»
«Yes, you should also orientate your body towards me and only look at me even if they talk to you.»
«But we are not teenagers and it would be very unnatural and rude towards others.»
«No, this is the only way to show people that you really love me for who I am.»
«So nobody will ever know that you actually made me sign a prenuptial agreement?»
«No, nobody needs to know that.»
«Who cares what people think?»
«Stop arguing with me, you must do as I say, otherwise you can return home alone.»
«Meili, please don't try to make a puppet of me.
You know very well that if you push me, I'll do it.»
We saw more of Shanghai and for the two following days we travelled in the limousine to Suzhou & Hangzhou. The next day we flew to Peking and was taken to another five-star hotel in another limousine. The first afternoon we visited the Tiananmen square and later on we met three of Meili's ex-colleagues and influential tv producers for dinner. She briefly mentioned my comic talent to them, but without elaborating further on it as it was only our very first meeting.

The next morning while having breakfast, she received a call and then she suddenly started to panic. After that frantic phone call, she told me to stop eating and follow her to our room because we had to leave immediately. We packed our suitcases in a hurry and went directly to the airport. Meanwhile she made a lot of phone calls, but despite me asking what was happening, she didn't explain anything to me. At the airport she bought two tickets for Chongqing and later on when we arrived there in the evening, a man who was waiting outside her house, handed her two tickets for Christchurch. I met her father and five members of her family and later on Meili showed me a few photos of her mother who had passed away a long time ago. I presented my gifts to her family and then we went out for dinner. We returned and went to bed late around two am and got up at five to run to the airport and escape to New Zealand. Hence our luxurious wedding reception, our honey moon around China and all her ambitious plans for a career for me as a comedian in Chinese television, had abruptly come to an end and we had spent one week in China, of which only about seven hours in her house.

Weeks later and against the advice of my step daughter, Meili finally agreed to talk about the Peking phone call:

«When I was a tv producer, I had a business partner who had got himself involved in some illegal activities.»

«What kind of illegal activities?»

«They say he owned a brothel in Shanghai and laundered the money to justify his huge income.»

«And you were never involved in any of it?»

«No, I didn't know anything until a while ago.»
«Why did we have to run away from China in such hurry after that phone call?»
«Because they told me he had just been arrested and I feared he would mention me as his accomplice.»
«Why would he want to involve you?»
«To receive a milder sentence.»
«How could he have done it without being able to proof it?»
«It's not about proofing; he would have defamed me.»
«He could have done it wherever you were.»
«Yes, but it was very inconvenient that they had to arrest him just as we were in China.»
«Were you two lovers?»
«No, I was married at the time.»
«Is he the person who often calls you?»
«No, that's enough with questions.»
«Was it him whom you met alone in Shanghai?»
«No.»
«Then who did you see that day? Tell me everything.»
«It's none of your business.»
«Yes, it is, I am your husband, but unlike me you deliberately hide many secrets from me.
I think he was the person whom you saw in Shanghai and the friend who paid all our expenses until Peking, right?»
«No that's enough.»
«Are you hiding in New Zealand?»
«No and I don't want to talk about it anymore.»
«And I don't know how you can expect me to trust you.»

Meili demanded my constant care and attention and I was always busy taking care of her every need like a babysitter.
I was still unemployed, so one day I asked her:
«How about your promise to lend me some money?»
«Let's sell my two houses and buy a nicer one.»
«Your houses need some work in order to get better prices.»
«Yes, I know, but what can we do?»
«Give me a few weeks and I will prepare them for sale.
Where would you like to buy a nicer house?»
«Let's go around the country and find a warmer place.»
«What a fantastic idea, okay let's do it.»
We travelled by car all over the country and then we returned to Nelson on top of the South Island, where a few days later Meili bought a beautiful house for two million dollars. But after having moved into the new home, her attitude changed drastically. She became stingy, started to treat me like a slave and showing an unfounded jealousy, she made me end my friendship with Sara. She also became malicious and very intrusive. She insisted to read my emails, picked up my phone and checked my messages before me and had an excessive interest in my bank accounts without ever revealing anything about herself to me.
One night just as we had gone to bed:
«Elias, why do you still refuse to give me maintenance?»
«I have already explained everything to you. I lost my income because of your promise to help me with a business and now I am spending all my savings which are drying up.»
«I am a traditional woman and I would like to receive money from my husband in the palm of my hand.»

«But you are very wealthy with many incomes in China.»
«I bought this beautiful house for us.»
«No, you bought it for yourself because I do not have right to anything, but contrary to your prenup agreement, I refurbished your two houses and also paid for all the material.»
«Lian and I think you should access your capital and furnish our house with vintage furniture.»
«I am sorry, I can't do that. I need that money to create my own business. Besides, it's against the terms of your agreement.»
«Don't worry; I will buy you a taxi.»
«No, I neither want your money nor becoming a taxi driver.»
«What do you want to do then?»
«Well, if you could manage to take care of yourself, I will look for any job that I could find. Meanwhile when the exchange rate becomes favorable, I will change my Kronor in dollars and buy the pastry café in the city.»
«No! If you don't want to do as I say, you have to leave now.» Stretching out her arm toward the door with irate.
«What are you saying? You mean… leaving you?»
«Yes! I can find another man tomorrow.
Get out of my house.»
I was shocked and left the bedroom and she locked the door, worrying that I might steal her jewelry collection while she slept. She wanted to put me on a tight leash, but I could no longer allow her to abuse me and ruin my finances. I packed and loaded almost all my personal belongings in the car and left the house, but given that it was very late, I had to spend a horrible night in my car in the driver's seat.

In the morning I drove to Christchurch to prepare for my return to Europe. But Meili kept calling me, crying and trying to make me return to her. Later on also Lian and her fiancé called me and told me how distressed Meili was, so I returned home to retry. However, this kept happening often and every time she became meaner. In the meantime not being able to find any job, I was forced to cash in my bank draft and lost almost twenty-five thousand dollars. That was a very hard blow and the miracle of my life had also turned into a nightmare after only three months of marriage. The last time she kicked me out, we agreed to file a joint divorce application with the City Council and then I also withdrew my sponsorship for her residency. Later on I went to Christchurch and after selling the car, I returned to Dublin where I had lived previously to join my brother Ervin and like many years before, I started working in his Italian restaurant. I could do it all, management, cashier, waiting, cooking and the bar, but I also did a lot of maintenance. Meili called me a few times at the restaurant, suggesting that we should retry while travelling in Europe, but I didn't want to return to her ever again. I just needed to wait a two-year period of separation before our marriage would dissolve automatically.

A nice place in Peru

I had recently thought about the Italian life style, so a few weeks later I moved to Florence and was astonished by the beauty of the city. I considered establishing a Bugatti boutique, so I had to learn functional Italian and as soon as possible. While staying in a small hotel, I met Eva from Wellington in New Zealand, who traveled in Europe without her husband. We got together visiting many incredible cites in the city, starting with Piazza del Duomo, the grand Cathedral of Santa Maria del Fiore, Giotto's Bell Tower and San Giovanni's baptistery. The next day we went to Piazza della Signoria and saw the Neptune Fountain, Palazzo Vecchio and the open-air gallery of the Loggia dei Lanzi displaying many magnificent statues like *Perseus* holding the decapitated head of *Medusa*. Another day we visited the Uffizi galleries and later on Palazzo Pitti, the largest museum complex in the city and the following day we enjoyed the Accademia Gallery and admired Michelangelo's *Il David*.

Eva also helped me find an apartment, but I didn't want to rent any of the luxurious homes on offer. So I decided to find a short-term rental and, in the meantime, keep looking for an economic place. One day we went to see a furnished studio apartment on the other side of the river Arno, very close to Palazzo Pitti and Ponte Vecchio, a beautiful medieval stone bridge and one of the most famous bridges in the world. I decided to rent the studio apartment and couldn't wait to start learning Italian.

A few days later however, I became sick with what I thought was a nasty pneumonia. I bought some over the counter medicine at the pharmacy, but my symptoms kept worsening. One late night I was in such critical condition that Eva had to take me to the emergency room at Santa Maria Novella hospital. After a short waiting time, I was called in the examination room and then a doctor who spoke good English entered:
«Hello, I am doctor Pieri. How do you feel?»
«Hello doctor, I feel exhausted, I have difficulties breathing with headache, shivers and a persistent cough.»
«Your pulse is accelerated and you have a fever.
Do you suffer from allergies or asthma?»
«No, I think I have pneumonia.»
«It's possible, but we have to verify it with a chest X-ray and some blood tests.
Pull up your shirt and keep taking deep breaths.
I hear a hissing sound in your lungs.»
Then they started taking blood samples for various tests and later on made me lie on a cot in the crowded hallway with other patients as they tried to find beds for us. In the meantime I had completely lost track of time, but I knew Eva was still sitting in the waiting room to hear from me. It wasn't until they were taking me to the radiology that I saw her asleep in a tiny chair in a very uncomfortable position and about to fall on the floor. I felt very sorry for her, so I asked a nurse to go to her and advise her that she could return to the hotel without me. A short time later while undergoing treatment with Ventolin in a nebulizer, doctor Pieri returned to me:

«Elias, we have a diagnosis for you.
You have what we call a walking pneumonia.»
«What do you mean by walking?»
«I mean permanent pneumonia or Bronchitis.»
«Really?»
«Yes, but don't worry, you can live with it.
Are you an Italian resident?»
«No, not yet.»
«We will keep you here for a few days, but you should return to your country as soon as possible for a long-term treatment.»
I was traumatized, it was the most terrible news of my life and I couldn't believe my bad luck. I had just arrived where my heart desired to be and I was about to fulfill one of my dreams, but this disease could have put everything in jeopardy. They treated me intensively for three days, but Eva never came to see me and by the time I was discharged from the hospital, she had already gone away. I considered returning to Dublin, but then I decided not to allow this disease to break my spirit and learn to manage it until I could access the Italian health care system as a resident. Like in all other EU countries, I was required to register with the municipality and show a source of income in Italy or to buy a health insurance to obtain a residency status. Normally it would have taken two-three weeks in most EU countries, but in Italy, it could have taken as long as three months and also required the applicant's registered and verified residential address. I had to find a home where I could put a nametag at the entrance of the building in anticipation of a random visit by the municipal police for the verification of my address.

I moved into the furnished studio apartment that Eva and I had found together and spent many hours cleaning it. There were many language schools in Florence, but I had already enrolled in *Il David Institute*, in the heart of the city, unaware of how the course of events there, would change my life forever.
On Friday of my first week at school, I left the class after the last lesson and approached a beautiful lady about 45 years old who smiled at me and introduced myself to her in English:
«Hi Elias, I am Olivia.»
«Nice to meet you, Olivia. Where do you come from?»
«From Switzerland and you?»
«Iranian born with Swedish and Australian citizenships.»
«You have been around. What are you doing in Italy?»
«I have just moved to Florence and intend to live here.»
«What a wonderful idea, it's really a beautiful city.»
«Yes of course. And you, what are you doing here?»
«I speak Spanish and I would like to learn also Italian.»
«How come you speak Spanish?»
«I live in South America. I have found a nice place in Peru.»
«How interesting! Seems like you have been around too.
Do you know there is a school trip this afternoon?»
«Yes, I know, we will go to *Fiesole* and I have already put my name in the list. Will you go too?»
«Yes sure, I love exploring new places.
Would you like to go to Luciano's for lunch?»
«No thanks, I eat at home.»
«Then see you this afternoon.»
«Okay, see you later.»

That afternoon we all gathered in front of the school and walked all the way to Piazza San Marco, but I did not approach Olivia. Then we took the bus to Fiesole and I still stayed away from her as she was busy talking to her friends. *"A nice place in Peru!",* I was curious and wondered if she was looking for love. It seemed like a great opportunity to start a relationship with her and maybe fall in love in Florence. I would have easily given up all my future plans in Italy for a beautiful love story with Olivia in Peru.
What an exciting adventure it would have been!

In Fiesole we walked uphill to the terrace that rises in the public gardens from where you can see the spectacular panorama of Florence. I soon realized that I couldn't breathe easily. When we reached the top of the walkway, I was so short of breath and felt so many twinges in my chest that I had to walk away from the group. But Olivia called me and gave her camera to another student to take a photo of the two of us with the magnificent city of Florence in the background. Then I walked away again without being able to exchange even a single word with her. I was really in agony because of the excruciating chest pain and trying to hide my tears, I decided to walk behind everybody else. Hence during the time it took to walk the tourist track, I had suffered from such a severe anguish that I had not been able to even throw a second glance at her. When we returned to Piazza Mino, Olivia and some students decided to stay there longer. I too wanted to stay to get to know her, but my condition was very unpredictable and I feared it could change into an emergency at any moment. I didn't want to involve Olivia in my problem.

I felt compelled to get on that bus and return to Florence in order to be closer to Santa Maria Novella hospital, where they already knew about my illness. I got on the bus and stood with my face towards the footpath, staring at Olivia who was at the bus stop in front of me looking back at me. She seemed puzzled, as if she couldn't quite understand why I had behaved in such a strange way and why I had tried to avoid her even for a chat. Perhaps she expected me to stay with her and I was hoping she could see from my gestures that I really did not want to leave. It was soon time to go when I heard the doors closing and the bus left the stop. My eyes were still fixed on her face and while the bus was making a U-turn in the piazza towards Florence, I turned around to see her. She was still looking in my direction. I went away from a beautiful woman, from her mysterious place in Peru and from everything that might have happened between us, if only I had been able to find out. I left Olivia behind without knowing anything about her, without being able to recognize her face and without leaving any trace of me. All that was left of us was just a photo in her camera and our brief memories from each other.

The illness

As expected, I spent a horrible weekend during which I decided to leave. The following Monday morning I went to the institute to inform the management that I had to interrupt my studies due to illness and few days later I returned to Dublin. I consulted my family doctor and she referred me to Peter O'Connor, a private pulmonologist who after doing a CT scan and a few blood tests, also diagnosed me with bronchitis:
«We must do a bronchoscopy and a bronchial wash.»
«Why, to clean the lungs?»
«Yes, but also to check the return fluid from the wash, to take a sputum sample to grow in laboratory in search of bacteria and to do a biopsy for cancer.»

An agonizing month later I went back for the final diagnosis:
«We have received the results of the sputum cultivation.
Your lungs are in fact infected with a very rare and fast-growing mycobacterium.»
«What?»
«Don't worry, it is not like it's cancer.»
«So the infection can be permanently cured, right?»

«Yes, but we have to do a long-term treatment to completely eliminate the mycobacterium in your lungs. I will prescribe you some antibiotics to try and then we will do the same tests every month to see if there has been a change.»
It was a more devastating news and I couldn't understand why I had been infected with a rare mycobacterium that normally lives in the soil. I soon remembered my extensive work in the gardens of Meili's houses as the most likely cause.

After months of tests and treatment, the pulmonologist told me:
«Looks like your situation has stabilized.»
«That's right, I've been feeling much better recently.
So the infection must have been eliminated?»
«Yes, but you should continue with the treatment for a few more months to make sure it won't repeat itself.»
«Yes sure. I think it would be better if I relocate to the warm and dry weather in Italy.»
«An excellent idea, but if your health should deteriorate again, you must come back to me right away.»
I returned to Il David Institute and after a few weeks I noticed my health was indeed deteriorating again. My violent cough and my breathlessness were coming back and I often burned with high fever. I felt devastated because it only meant that the infection was reoccurring. I had already concluded my life twice in Ireland and did not want to return there again. I didn't know what to do, but in the end, I decided to complete the Irish treatment and wait for my Italian residency regardless of the time it would take to access the Italian health care system.

Most of the students who attended the institute for no more than two weeks, were young and went out every evening. Given the symptoms of my illness and despite the pressure from some teachers, I couldn't anymore participate in every school event and had to stay away from people. I couldn't walk at a steady pace for more than a few minutes at a time or ascend stairs even one level without hyperventilating. I struggled with insomnia and couldn't take deep breaths because of my aching lungs. I also felt repulsive, especially in public, because I had to constantly cough and empty my lungs. It was as if I was breathing through a tiny straw and not knowing if I could make love to a woman, I had also lost all my self-esteem.

The school had only female teachers, all young and beautiful. They were also very kind and their voices sounded like music to my ears. I had already finished the two grammar books during my treatment in Dublin and I was so fascinated by Italian that I devoted all my time to study. Chiara was nice to me and she was the first teacher who was worried about me burying myself under the grammar books, so one day she asked me in English:
«Why aren't you as happy and cheerful as the other students?»
«Because I am fifty-two years old and not twenty-five.»
«Why aren't you looking for a woman?»
«Well, because I am very sick.»
I was hoping she would ask what was wrong with me, but:
«Oh yeah, I know. There is a bug going around.»
Chiara didn't want to hear any more excuses and from that day on, she started treating me as if I was a snob.

In another occasion, also teacher Laura asked me during the conversation class:
«Elias, did you go out last night?»
«No, I was home studying?»
«Why aren't you looking for a girlfriend?»
I wanted to tell her that I really liked having a girlfriend if I was healthy, but I couldn't manage it in my Italian. I should have told her I was sick, instead scrolling down a long imaginary list that reached the floor, I tried to show her that for the moment, having a woman was the last of my priorities. But because she reacted as if I had deeply insulted her, I think she thought I was a sexist and considered women inferior.

Then there was Stella, a gorgeous and very charismatic thirty-two-year-old Italian lady, whom I considered only a teacher. She was very confident and charming and dressed elegantly. I soon noticed that I was getting the kind of attention from Stella to which I wasn't able to respond. She sometimes read my story writing assignments for the class, often used my name in her examples, like: *"Elias loves Stella"* and almost always looked into my eyes as if we were alone and so on. Her seductive smiles, her deep gazes that penetrated my soul and her body language suggested attraction, so I decided to act passively and resist her charm until she got tired and gave up on me. Nevertheless, my indifferent attitude didn't work and her unwanted attention soon became intense and more open. After a while I realized she was arousing wonderful feelings in me, but I didn't know what to do to avoid becoming emotionally attracted to her.

One day after asking us if we liked a crowded sandy beach or a rocky secluded one, she wanted to know:
«Why do you prefer a deserted beach to a crowded one?»
«To avoid seeing all those fat and ugly bodies.»
Then she turned to her side and put her hourglass-shaped body in a sensual position with a sultry gaze and a seductive smile:
«Do you like this body?»
She took my breath away, but I managed to react indifferently, shaking my head. On another occasion when complaining about my noisy neighbors, she offered me a room in her apartment and kept staring at me with a flirtatious smile. I didn't make any comment until the end of the lesson when she said that the room was actually too small.

I was developing feelings for Stella and couldn't understand why she would want to play with my heart. I also had to look for a quiet neighborhood and move. So I made an appointment with Luca, an associate of Il David Institute who had previously taken us to the seaside villages of *Cinque Terre*. He showed me a nice two-story apartment that I couldn't afford and then we went for coffee. I was sad and had tears in my eyes as I was looking at Luca to decide if I should confide in him or not. In the meantime, he had realized that I was about to tell him a secret. I finally broke my silence and told him that I had developed feelings for a teacher who had shown a lot of unwanted interest in me and accidentally mentioned Stella's name. Luca looked very puzzled and to my astonishment, he suddenly cried out in disbelief:
«A woman?»

Then he asked why this was tormenting me so much and I had to explain my reality to him. But Luca didn't have any advice to offer me and I still didn't know what to do with Stella.

Isabel, one day we met in the conversation class, but your Italian was much more advanced. I remember you complaining about how couples often fought and you believed men always told a bunch of lies, while I and a young Greek were trying to convince you that you were very wrong. You expressed many prejudices towards men that day, but I didn't notice your absence when the next day you were moved to an advanced class.

I attended the institute every day and had to stay at home in the evenings for the local police to knock on my door and verify my address. I was also dealing with a traumatic crisis and my world was falling apart because of my ever-declining physical abilities. I struggled with anxiety, anger, denial, guilt and an immense sense of loss for who I used to be just a few months earlier. I was still alive, but life as I knew it, had changed drastically. I had been condemned to an existence of pain and agony and there was nothing else that I could do, except committing suicide. It was necessary to go through the various stages of grief before accepting my reality. I had to act stoically in public or avoid all social events so as not to inflict my pain and suffering on others. During the breaks, I had to go to Piazza della Repubblica near the school to discreetly manage my symptoms, but because no one knew why, they considered me asocial and believed I went out just to avoid socializing with them.

One morning returning from the square very depressed and deeply lost in my thoughts, I noticed I was a little late. I entered the deserted corridor and passed by the first classroom with its door open. Then I turned left and after a few steps just as I was about to enter my classroom, I heard a female voice:
«Hi Elias.»
I stepped back and looking to my right, I saw a woman whom I didn't recognize cheerfully smiling at me with radiant eyes:
«It's me, Isabel.»
Then stepping on your toes, you did a flawless pirouette which made your hair fly in the air and lifted up your dress a little. You had dyed your long hair in beige blonde with brighter highlights, wore a lite makeup and the glasses had disappeared. You were dressed in an adorable light blue dress and an elegant pair of low-heeled shoes. Absolutely gorgeous!
I was astonished. You were there and you were very real, a truly magical moment during which you managed to stimulate all my senses with the hint of a sweet story that could have followed. A lovely woman whose charm had attracted the attention of an indifferent man in such stunning way in a deserted corridor. Suddenly time had stood still and I couldn't take my eyes off you. I was admiring you from top to bottom when moments later I had to allow Stella who was coming from the opposite side, to pass behind me in the narrow hallway carrying some books to your class. I really wanted to approach you, but I wasted that delightful moment and entered my classroom without smiling or saying anything to you. It wasn't rudeness; I could not even have friends, let alone a girlfriend.

But during the lesson, I couldn't stop thinking about what had just happened in the corridor; you had impressed me by taking such a charming initiative. I suddenly wanted to run to you and it would have been enough to just take your hand and run away with you wherever you wanted to go, but instead, I had ignored you. I considered inviting you to lunch, but then I remembered my situation and decided not to drag you into my pathetic life. After the last lesson I went to lunch, alone, and a few minutes later I saw you and your friends entering Luciano's trattoria. You saw me and you smiled at me. I on the other hand, against my will, stayed away from you observing you discretely.

The evening of the tenth of August, the night of the shooting stars, hundreds of people would go to the feast of San Lorenzo to eat pasta with tomato sauce, watermelon and yogurt offered by the central market operators and street vendors. We gathered in front of the school around eight and walked to Piazza San Lorenzo. When we arrived there, most of the students spread out in the square waiting for the event to begin, while I chatted with three young guys standing around. You and your friends were sitting on the steps of San Lorenzo Basilica, observing us. Sometime later Irina, your Serbian friend, took a picture of me and the three guys and then you approached me with a smile. I had already tried to avoid you several times that evening, but I was delighted to see you coming to me. Maybe you were still interested in me or perhaps you just wanted to have a chat. Then the three young students walked away, leaving us alone and we started talking despite my very limited Italian:

«Hello Isabel.»
«Hello Elias, I am happy you could join us this time.»
«Thanks, I thought I needed a break.
It's a lovely evening.»
«Yes, and this is a wonderful event.»
I needed to justify my strange behavior, hoping to discourage you about me:
«Isabel, I would like to share something with you.»
«Yes, what is it?»
«I am actually very sick.»
«What is wrong with you?»
«I have a serious chronic lung disease and it is so horrible that I want to kill myself.»
«No, you shouldn't talk like that.
I too have a serious medical problem that bothers me a lot.»
«What is the matter with you?»
«It's a feminine problem.
My mother thinks I should operate, but I am very scared.»
«Why? Is it dangerous?»
«No, it's just that I don't like surgeries at all because of the risks of complications.»
«What are you going to do then?»
«I don't know, but I will have to decide soon.»
I was really amazed because that was a clear sign of trust which brings closeness. I admired your honesty and transparency and from that moment on, I liked you even more.
Then I suddenly started to feel strong twinges in my chest:
«Excuse me Isabel, now I am really in agony.»

«Why, what happened?»
«My lungs hurt when I breathe more air to talk or walk.
I have to sit down and rest for a while.»
«It's okay, go and rest and then come back.»
You had shown me sincerity, the finest moral virtue in life and the confession of your little secret and your kind words had gone straight to my heart. I walked away from you and sat on the low stone ledge of the Basilica facade to rest. But I wanted so much to get back to you, I wanted to run my fingers through your hair, to study your face, to know the color of your eyes and hear your sweet voice. I desired to hug you, to smell the scent of your skin and to tell you how long I had been thinking about you, but most of all, I wanted to listen to your heart.

I couldn't cope with loneliness and the sense of emptiness, but I felt unworthy of any woman because of my hopeless situation. I believed no woman would ever want to be with me if she found out about the state of my health. I was sitting there for quite a while crying discreetly and struggling to decide if it was best to let you go before I got too attached to you. A while later when I returned to the crowd, you were gone. I felt so lost that I wanted to shout out your name and find you, except that it didn't make much sense. I could only offer you my love, because not only I didn't have my health, I was also older than you. So I decided to avoid you and joined other students, trying to pretend as if I was having fun. In reality I was very restless within knowing that the woman I liked, was somewhere in the square just a few short steps away from me.

During the break on a Friday, there was another gathering on the roof-top terrace of the school and we all could eat delicious watermelon offered by the school management. I took a slice and sat next to the young Greek and when I saw you coming to me, I got up and walked towards you:
«Hi Elias.»
«Hi Isabel, how are you?»
«Good thanks. How are your studies going?»
«It's not easy, I have to study many hours a day at home.»
«Today is my last day here and I return to Spain on Monday.»
I knew you wanted to go out with your friends for the weekend and maybe you wanted me to come with you, but there was no point because I couldn't have you. I had nothing else to say and I was just standing in front of you looking at the pavement, until you turned around and walked away without saying a word. That's when something inside me snapped. That Friday evening I went out, alone, and dragged my feet for a while in the streets of Florence, reflecting on you and another lost opportunity.

Every day I arrived early and went on the roof-top terrace waiting for the first lesson to begin. One morning as I sat at a table and enjoyed the cool of the early morning, someone came and stood between me and the horizon, obscuring my rays of sun.
It was Stella!
My heart began to throb faster and then it was filled with delight. She was usually late, so her early arrival took me off guard as if she had materialized from my mind. We greeted each other and then she sat next to me, exposing herself to the sun.

By now I had turned my eyes away from the horizon and moved them on her face that this close, was a splendor. She removed her hairband and gracefully shaking her head from side to side, twirled her wavy black hair that quickly fell over her shoulders and then she put on her sunglasses. The sun was now shining on Stella, reflecting her extraordinary beauty in the universe, while I was so hypnotized that I didn't even want to blink an eye so as not to miss a single moment of all the love that she was. I couldn't look into her eyes and she remained silent, as if she knew she had captured my soul, as if she was listening to my lonely heart. Stella was glowing next to me, but in comparison, she felt light years away. I cherished her and I had so much to tell her, but she would have never known anything. Moments later another student arrived and everything suddenly vanished into the thin air like a bubble bursting.

I was very ashamed for my illness and didn't want to reveal my secret to anyone, but I could no longer cope with what Stella was provoking me. So one day I decided to tell the entire class about my illness in order to change Stella's attitude towards me and in doing so, also explain the reason for my very enigmatic behavior. Although I had obvious and frequent symptoms, Stella was very surprised to learn how ill I was and advised me to immediately seek medical help. I briefly explained my efforts in search of a cure, but she wasn't aware of the complexity of my lung infection and I didn't want to spoil everyone's mood with medical details. After that day, I was hoping she would treat me just like any other student, but I was wrong.

On a Friday she told us she would go on holiday for a week and advised us to go to a local concert the same evening. She was very cheerful and didn't teach us much grammar. She played the song *"Choose me"* from a CD player and started dancing and singing along with Gianna Nannini. Then she wrote the song title on the whiteboard as she stared at me smiling.
So when the lesson finished, I tried to hurry out:
«Elias!»
I stopped and turned toward her:
«This was my very last lesson with you. Don't you want to say good-bye to your teacher before leaving the school?»
She walked towards me with her arms open along her sides and an anticipating look as if she wanted a hug. I couldn't hug Stella once without wanting to do it again and again. Staring at her, I lost myself in her hazel eyes and when I got myself together:
«Yes of course. But I will be here when you come back and I would never leave the school without first thanking everyone.»
Then I left and soon regretted not hugging her.

I hadn't still finished my studies, but no one knew I wanted to study for another two months starting from the following week. However, Stella's beauty and charm tormented me and I had to keep her out of my heart. I considered changing school, but I liked its location in a nice building with a lift. I decided to go to the concert that Friday evening and find a way to change Stella's impressions of me. I went to the *Fortezza da Basso* and entered the venue as soon as they opened the gates in the early evening and I had to wait for her for many grueling hours.

Later on just before the concert began, I saw her approaching a young man about her age near the stage and taking his hand, she turned around scanning the crowd, as if she was looking for someone. Then she stopped when she saw me looking at her from a short distance, but none of us made a nod in recognition. She seemed puzzled and maybe expected me to approach her, but I didn't want her to think I had gone there to see her. I had my usual violent cough and I had to move around constantly so as not to disturb the crowd. Later on when she saw me again at a distance, she waited for a while and continued to look in my direction to encourage me to approach her and greet her. But I decided to ignore her in order to change what she thought of me without having to talk to her about us. Although I felt very relieved to have found an opportunity to behave arrogantly, I hated myself for disrespecting her. Sometime later I returned home as soon as they left the location together.

One day I received another email from Sara. Having lived with the Australian man for a while, she had mentally grown up and now she could appreciate everything I had done for her during our marriage and after the divorce. She had apologized many times before, expressing her great regret for not having been a participatory and supportive wife, but this time:

Hi Elias

David has told me Florence is one of the most beautiful cities in the world. I am very excited and I would like to come to Florence because I want to be with you. See you soon.

Sara

It had already past three years since our divorce, but I would have given her another chance. However, I wasn't able to take care of myself and I wasn't even sure I'd survive the disease, let alone if I could rekindle the romance with my ex-wife.

I had to stop her from coming to me:

Beautiful Sara

I have never stopped loving you because as you know my love for you will never die. I am sincerely honored for your desire to join me and I would like to have you by my side again, but I'm afraid it won't be a good idea.

I feel unworthy of you because of a rare lung infection that has caused me bronchitis.

Please forgive me, I have no other choice but to suppress my wish and all your feelings and ambitions for our reunion and I hope you can move on without me.

With love

Elias

Lost love

Two weeks later, Stella hadn't still returned and I was wondering if she had extended her vacation or if she had fallen sick. One afternoon after lunch at Luciano's as I was passing by the school block on my way home, I heard familiar voices on the side street and saw teachers Chiara and Laura talking to a woman obscured by Laura. I had no reason to bother them and crossed the small intersection without a second look.

A couple of days later I began to think that Stella's absence must have been caused by me, but I couldn't justify her overreaction. What possible significance did I have in Stella's life?
Then reflecting on that afternoon at the side of the school block, I realized the third woman I hadn't been able to see, must have been Stella telling her friends how bad I had behaved that Friday night at the concert. I didn't know if they had noticed that I had seen them, but if so, my attitude must have seemed very hateful to all of them, because I had seen Stella again and I had ignored her also in front of her colleagues.
Even more contemptuous!
But why had they met outside the school?

Within a few days after this event, I noticed not only almost all teachers had stopped greeting me, they even treated me badly. I was a model student, but I had been branded asocial and now an outcast. Some teachers had lost all respect for me and despite the astonishment of other students, completely ignored me during the lessons as if I didn't exist. It seemed as if they had developed more prejudice against me and wanted to force me to leave the school. I could understand their reactions and because the three teachers had met outside the institute, it was obvious that Stella must have been dismissed or maybe had resigned for refusing to see me. Many times I wanted to ask about her, but apart from some students, no one else would even mention her name. I had a guilty conscience and regretted the way I had treated her, but I didn't think there was anything I could do to rectify the situation. The damage had already been done and it was clear that Stella would never return even if I left. The atmosphere had become unbreathable for me as I could no longer cope with the mistreatments and deal with my guilt for unintentionally causing her to lose her job.

My studio had only one window that opened to a very small and enclosed courtyard without a view of the sky. Therefore many days after lunch at Luciano's near the school, I returned to the bright and airy classroom on the beautiful roof-top terrace to do the homework during the hottest hours of the afternoon. One day I noticed Claudio, the school director coming up to me, but as soon as we saw each other, he turned around and went back down without saying anything.

I thought he wanted me to leave so I decided to go home. Then as I was passing in front of his office, he ran out in a hurry and seemed troubled as if I had done something very wrong:
«Why don't you want a woman?»
I felt a bit annoyed for having to always explain myself to others, but because I was depressed and he didn't know anything about my situation, I couldn't answer him and left. I wish I had stayed with Claudio to confide in him and see if I could find Stella to explain everything and to apologize. Unfortunately my sudden illness had affected all aspects of my personality so much that I wasn't lucid and I didn't behave rationally.

The following Monday, the third week of Stella's absence, I was very much heartbroken by remorse and felt so bad because of the humiliations that in the end I succumbed to the pressure. I left the grammar class a few minutes before the break and then the conversation class only five minutes after its beginning. I had to walk out of the school without saying a word to anyone, because I knew nobody would have any empathy or compassion for me. The same day, also my landlord advised me he wanted to sell his studio while I was still waiting for my address to be verified by the local police for my residency status. I had to find a new apartment, reregister and change the new address in the municipality office and wait even longer. I also had to enroll in another school to continue learning Italian, but I was physically and emotionally exhausted and didn't have the necessary energy and enthusiasm. My life was falling apart again and I couldn't even recognize myself for the way I behaved.

I had hurt Stella's feelings and ruined a few chances in finding a partner not only with Olivia and you, but also with two other beautiful ladies, one from Ukraine and the other from Poland. All my love for Italy had turned to dust and had blown away by the wind and all my future plans had been eroded by the rain to disappear where the water flows. I had failed miserably and had to run away from Italy with a broken spirit and a shattered heart.

I found another private pulmonologist in Dublin, Gerard Reilly, and three months later when he was examining me for the last time, he declared:
«Good news Elias, this time they haven't found any trace of the mycobacterium in your lungs.»
«This has happened also before.»
«Yes, I know, but we have to trust the test results.»
«So you think I am cured now?»
«Well relatively. Nevertheless, you have to finish the treatment and use the nebulizer every day for the physiotherapy.»
I didn't know what to believe, but I was hoping it was the last time. However, due to my damaged lungs and the Irish weather, I couldn't live in Dublin. I was also demoralized and couldn't find inner serenity because of my immense sense of guilt for Stella. I wished I could undo the pain I had caused her and let her know what I really thought of her. I decided to return to Florence, look for any available job and try to find Stella to clarify things to her and ask her to forgive me. A few days later I boarded a ferry in Rosslare in county Wexford to Roscoff and after crossing all of France, I arrived in Florence with a mission.

I rented a studio in Montelupo Fiorentino, a small community in the metropolitan city of Florence and almost every day drove to Scandicci where Stella used to live. I was hoping to find her by chance in the town center, but I had no luck. Sometimes I walked around Il David Institute, hoping to see a teacher I knew and discreetly ask her about Stella. I couldn't find work and despite continuing with the treatment, the lung infection kept advancing, forcing me to buy any other antibiotic without a prescription in order to manage my horrible symptoms, but all in vain. A month later I was in such a critical condition that I had to frantically conclude my life in Italy and drive to Hamburg, where one night my younger brother had to call an ambulance because I couldn't breathe. I had a very tormenting existence that I could no longer tolerate and I was convinced that I was terminally ill. A few days later, I left all my possessions behind and flew to Dublin to start looking for a cure wherever I could, or die trying.

I spent the next three years in absolute desolation, homeless, unemployed and extremely sick with horrendous symptoms, in and out of ambulances, emergency rooms, public hospitals and private clinics. I had to risk further contamination by having to travel about twenty times back and forth to Frankfurt, Hamburg, Stockholm, Dublin, Brescia, Milan, Verona, Lucca, Florence, Brisbane and Nelson to visit various specialists and alternative treatments, including ozone therapy and homeopathy. When I had spent almost everything that I had left of my life savings, I realized that none of the antibiotics available at the time could eliminate the infection once and for all.

Once when I was in Frankfurt to visit Nikos Diamandis, a Greek pulmonologist, Sara called me on Skype:
«Hi Sara, what a pleasant surprise.»
«Hi Elias, how is your health?»
«it's better, thanks. You are beautiful as ever.»
«No, I am older with some wrinkles and a few gray hairs.»
«Yes, but you are aging gracefully.»
«You look good with the beard.»
«I don't like it, but I don't want to shave every day.
How is David doing?»
«He is fine, but he often camps with the tourists in the forest, so sometimes we don't see each other for days.»
«I am sorry. Have you introduced him to your family?»
«Yes, we have been to Tokyo and he has met everyone.»
«Then he must have finally proposed?»
«Yes, he has, and we will have a traditional Japanese wedding in the same Shinto shrine where we got married.»
«Wonderful, congratulations!»
«Thanks.»
«What type of a man is he?»
«He is very relaxed and doesn't know how to fix things around the house as you used to do.»
«How is your work?»
«It's still okay, but I don't like my colleagues.»
«Why? What do they do?»
«I am fed up hearing them talking behind each other's back.»
«It doesn't matter, it's very common in workplaces.»
«How is your brother Ervin?»

«He is always tired because as usual he works seven days a week without ever taking a vacation. But the good news is that my niece Lisa, will soon marry Ronan.»
«Oh how nice, I think they will make a good couple.»
«Yes, let's hope so. How is your dad?»
«He is getting very old and recently has serious problems with his eye sight.»
«I am very sorry.»
«He often asks about you and still records your birthday in his calendar.»
«Ah, that's very sweet of him.
Tell me Sara, are you happy?»
...
«Yes, I am happy, but David is not you.
Elias I am sorry for the way I used to behave before.»
«No, there is no need to apologize. We've already talked about this before; I wasn't a perfect husband either.»
«I have changed so much; I wish you had given me more time to see things clearly.»
«I did Sara. I stayed with you for almost nine years.
Please don't reflect on the past and instead think about the lady you have become today.»
«I have been so lucky to have met you in my life.»
«Sara, loving you was a dream come true and as you know, you will always have a place in my heart.»
«And you will remain in mine eternally.»
«My best wishes for the wedding and greet everyone.»
«Bye Elias, you too greet your family.»

I led a lonely life and lived in the past, so I needed inner strength to cope with the adversity and to preserve my sanity. Many times I almost lost the battle simply because I couldn't even complete a short emergency call due to asphyxiation. But even though the infection was still advancing, I had found an extra ordinary way to survive spiritually thanks to the beautiful memories of the last delightful encounter in my life. I started to reflect on you Isabel, and on the few events that involved you from the moment you had attracted my attention in Florence. I meditated every day on you and everything that you meant to me. A precious memory that had soon turned into a vital spiritual strength for my mind and an emotional support for my heart as my only lifeline in solitude and despair.

You were my only companion and you always returned to my mind with open arms and stood by my side during my darkest hours, comforting me. I closed my eyes and called your name for every breath that I thought was my last and you appeared out of nowhere as my guardian angel, you gave me new breath and brought me back from imminent death. I had put you on a high pedestal and admired you as my ideal woman. A very powerful affection that had come to life and grown in me on its own, based only on my impressions of you. Reflecting on you strengthened my soul with spiritual stamina as you crawled steadily from my mind into my heart. I was developing wonderful feelings for a woman I didn't know well and I would've never seen again while expecting to die soon, but I never felt being all alone.
This was the only way I could cope and survive.

I soon realized that I had finished another fruitless nine-months treatment by Maria Nelson, a Swedish pulmonologist, when my symptoms began to recur. Aware that I could die within a few months, I decided to move to Australia, my other patria, to stay away from the family in order to save them the grief and to forget everything and everybody. I had found another specialist, Harry Jones in Brisbane who after having studied my medical records, couldn't understandably promise me a miracle cure. I began yet another treatment with terrible side effects and considered the idea of finding and handling a snake in the wild, or just getting lost in the vast Australian outback to finish it all if the symptoms of my disease got even worse.

But I had a rare and yet beautiful love story that I wished to leave behind as the greatest inspiration of my life before attempting suicide. An uncommon love for a woman who had attracted me emotionally and then despite her absence, had kept growing in me and had inspired my soul towards pure spirituality. An extra ordinary love that during the peak of my illness had turned into the contemplation of the divine and the supreme beauty in a platonic sense, the most romantic and sublime form of love. Although I could have easily written this story in my functional English, I decided to put it in writing in my fragmentary Italian as the only language we both spoke and titled it *Lost love*. It took me about three months to complete this story that despite its grammatical errors, made me feel privileged. In the meantime going through so many wonderful emotions, I missed you so much that I just couldn't stop thinking about you.

I felt well by the time I had completed the Australian treatment, but I still wasn't sure if the infection had been totally eradicated. In July of that year, I returned to Dublin and decided to finally join Facebook only to proudly share my story with everyone. *Lost Love* was the short original version of this very novel which was a tribute to you Isabel, to show my great appreciation for your good karma and compassion in Florence and for keeping me alive for three years. I published it on the Timeline page of Il David Institute, where we had met and hoped to find you and thank you.

Finding you

My heart stopped for a moment when the next day I got an email from Irina in Serbia with two photos of you and one of me and the other three students from the night of the shooting stars in Florence. She had written that you had already read *Lost love* and intended to contact me. Oh my God! Had I really found you? The next day you sent me a friendship request on Facebook and that same evening we started chatting, but you didn't know I had to use an online translator almost for every sentence to be able to communicate with you in Italian:
"Good evening Isabel, how is it going?"
"Good evening Elias, I am fine. How are you?"
"I am extremely emotional."
"Why?"
"Because I can't believe I am actually chatting with you.
Thanks a lot for contacting me."
"You're welcome. Where are you?"
"I am in Dublin! How about you?"
"I live in Rubí, near Barcelona."
"What have you been doing since we met in Florence?"
"Nothing special, what are you doing in Dublin?"
"I work for my brother, but I would like to relocate to Italy."
"Why?"
"Because I love Italy, but also because of the Irish weather.
What have you done for your medical problem?
Did you do the surgery?"
"How do you know about that?"

"You told me during the feast of San Lorenzo in Florence."
"Oh yeah, that's right. Yes, I did the surgery a couple of years ago and thank God, everything went well."
"Great! Do you know that Irina has sent me two photos of you?"
"Yes, she told me."
"You are really cute."
"I don't know, I don't feel that way."
"Why? What is the matter?"
"I feel a bit fat and old."
"No, you are not fat and definitely not old."
During other evenings we described our lives and our families. We used to chat every night, for hours, and once you wrote:
"I actually lost my job about a year ago."
"I am very sorry. What happened?"
"They closed the wool factory where I used to work."
"Can't you find another job?"
"No, as you know these days there aren't many opportunities."
"What are you going to do?"
"I have to wait until they reopen the factory."
"But it could take years."
"Yes, I know, but I have no other choice."
. . .
"Would you like to live in Dublin for a while?"
"I don't know.
I have never thought about moving to another country."
"But what if you can find a good job?'"
"I speak very little English."
"I can teach you and you can also go to school."

"What kind of job are you talking about?"
"My brother has an Italian restaurant and an Indian restaurant. When your English becomes good enough, you can start as a waitress and then work as a manager in any of the restaurants."
"But I don't know how to manage a restaurant."
"Don't worry, we will teach you everything."
. . .
"I don't know, I am not sure if I would be capable."
"Of course you would. Think about it and let me know."
I was dying to see you as soon as possible and I knew we could have made video calls if I didn't have to use an online translator to communicate with you. So during our next chat I wrote:
"I would like to see you, Isabel."
"Why?"
"Isn't it obvious?"
"Okay it is, but maybe not yet."
"Why not?"
"Because it's too early."
"Of course not! This isn't about a blind date; we already know each other."
Then you sent me a photo:
"Wow, is this you?"
"No it's my granny."
"You are absolutely gorgeous."
"Why don't you send me a photo?"
"I don't have any other photo except the one in my profile."
"How old is this photo?"
"About six years old.

"Send me a selfie, otherwise I will cancel our friendship."
"Are you serious?"
"Yes I am."
"Okay, I don't do selfies, but I'll send you a recent photo. So we can meet soon?"
"I don't know, I am not looking for a relationship."
That's okay, I just feel this impelling need to see you in person. What do you say?"
"Well, okay."
"Excellent! I will organize myself and let you know soon."
I asked my brother to take a picture of me, but I couldn't figure out why it was important if you weren't looking for a relationship. You would have celebrated your 45th birthday in September of that year and I wanted to make it unforgettable for you.
So during our next chat:
"Would you like to have dinner with me in Paris the evening of your birthday?"
"In Paris?"
"Yes, have you ever been there?"
"No never, but no thanks."
"Why not?"
"We don't know each other well enough."
"We'll have a few days before the trip to get to know each other better and then you can have your own room in Paris."
"No, I would never travel with a stranger."
"Well, then bring your mother with you if you can't trust me."
Hahaha! No thanks, I don't think so."
"I leave the invitation open in case you change your mind."

I was over the moon and felt blessed, because not only against all odds I was still alive, but I had also been able to find you. I would have met you soon and I was willing to do whatever it took to gain your complete trust.

A week later I flew to Barcelona twelve days before your birthday to make us feel more united for the trip to Paris and took the train for Rubí. The next morning I went out in search of flowers, but I couldn't find any. Then we met in front of my hotel which by chance was only about 3 minutes' walk from your building. I saw you wearing a nice white summer blouse, a brown miniskirt and a pair of sandals. I was nervous, but I didn't feel euphoric because I had to put you to the test before you could confirm yourself as the greatest love of my life. We kissed each other on the cheeks and headed to your apartment where I offered you my presents and then we went to the city. It was soon clear that I was not able to express myself in Italian the way I wanted and therefore I was very frustrated.

In the evening as we walked back from a local restaurant, you were proudly telling me about the compliments for *Lost love* by your Spanish friends who knew me from Il David Institute. I was so full of joy and happiness that I couldn't even take my eyes off you. So instead of walking next to you, I walked backwards and kept myself in front of you all the way to your building with the need to often look over my shoulders to see where I was going. Arriving at your building, you invited me up for a few minutes and then insisted that I confided in you:

«Elias, tell me about your feelings for me.»
«Come again?»
«Tell me what you feel for me.»
«You want to know what I feel for you, now?»
«Yes, I do.»
...
«Well! As you already know, I have been very fond of you ever since I saw your dance in the school corridor in Florence.»
«Yes, but what do you feel for me? Tell me the right words.»
«The right words? Come on.
Okay, there's no other way to say it.
I think I love you for what little I know you.»
«I on the other hand would like to fall in love in a natural way.»
«Yes, I agree and surely I didn't expect you to already have feelings for me.»
«But you aren't my type, just as you wouldn't like every woman. Do you understand?»
«Yes, I do.»
That wasn't what I expected to hear and I couldn't understand why you had agreed to see me if you didn't like me at all. I had already lost all my self-esteem because of the illness and now I was not even your type. I believed you because I thought you were sincere and I had to respect your opinion. I had acted like a fool, abandoning everything and running to you so fast. At that point I was embarrassed and considered myself an intruder. So I decided to apologize to you, leave and never bother you again, but before I did it, you told me we could meet the next day.
I agreed because I still wanted to find a way to thank you.

The next morning someone called you while you were showing me the photos of your trip to Istanbul and soon the conversation turned into a heated discussion. I realized you were talking about me because you kept repeating the word *Fantasía*, ridiculing me. You talked on the phone for about half an hour, after which you apologized without giving me any explanation.

In the evening when we had returned to your apartment, I was baffled when you went and put on your tiny shorts. I was sitting next to you on your only couch with my body a little twisted to face you and you were showing me your bare legs in various positions and looked at me with a flirtatious smile, making me believe that touching you was up to me. I had to earn your trust before the trip to Paris, but it seemed as if you were looking for sex. Maybe you wouldn't have felt comfortable enough traveling with me and wanted to get to know me your way. Of course I wanted to touch you and examine every single curve on your naked body, but not before getting to know each other a little emotionally. I was confused and didn't know how to interpret your conduct. I didn't know if you were testing my respect for you or if you wanted to check my virility this quickly. Moments later pretending to be sleepy, you asked me to leave.

The next afternoon we went to Sabadell and you took me to a nice department store to try, as an excuse, a Dolce & Gabbana perfume. Then you suggested that I should buy nicer clothing because we were about to meet some of your close friends.
I wish you had told me that much earlier.

I had brought a large suitcase full of nice clothes and shoes, but because I had been discouraged by you, I wore casual clothing instead. I didn't buy anything and despite a few phone calls, you deliberately delayed the appointment with your friends long enough that in the end we didn't meet anybody, so you wouldn't be embarrassed. Later on in the café of *Parc de Catalunya* you told me you still had nostalgia for your thirty-five-year-old ex and didn't know what to do. That was another serious concern which would've made the situation complicated. But I couldn't give up easily and before I knew, I had decided to show more courage for love. I still didn't know you and it was neither the right time nor the right place to make you feel how extraordinary my love was, but it was a touching moment and I was overly sentimental. So when we were leaving the park, I stopped you due to an incoercible impulse and very emotional:

«Isabel, I thought about you every day of the last three years and by now you have become an inseparable part of me.

I don't think you realize what you mean to me and I don't believe anybody could ever love you as much as I do.»

«Hmm, I have had many men who have loved me even more.» You said laughing at me.

I don't know what happened to me, it felt devastating, but I didn't want to pretend it didn't matter. You were once again ridiculing my love, but this time you hurt my feelings so brutally that I felt my soul leaving my body, making me collapse on some steps in the park. I sat there, looking up into your eyes in disbelief and felt so much anxiety that I was shaking like a leaf while my silent tears ran down my cheeks.

Meanwhile, you were standing in front of me looking down at me with a sarcastic smile full of satisfaction and victory, cynical and devoid of any empathy. Your cruel behavior was far beyond what I expected from you. Then while still laughing at me:
«Enough crying, let's go.»
I had to get up and follow you as you started to walk away.
I felt so mortified that I took a few steps away from you in protest and turned my head to the other side to hide my tears. Then I stopped with my shoulders hanging, my head down and my eyes closed as if I had just surrendered after another lost battle. Moments later I approached you sitting on a bench and deeply immersed in your thoughts:
«What do you want Isabel?»
«I want a good life; I don't want to work anymore.
I want financial security.»
...
«Well, I don't have much, but I can offer you all I have.
Here you are!»
I gently threw my wallet on your lap which accidentally landed on your groin, making you push it lower down on your miniskirt. After a few moments of silence, you handed over the wallet and we returned to Rubí in your car.

I fully expressed my instinctive desire to provide for you and paid for everything every time we went out. I also treated you like a lady, but whenever I wanted to touch you affectionately, you would withdraw your hand or any time I attempted to give you a hug or a little goodbye kiss on the cheek, you refused.

Because you couldn't identify yourself with the woman in *Lost love* and justify my feelings, you mocked my affection for you. You showed arrogance with smiles and because we had never made love, you considered my feelings as fantasies. You did not realize that because of my long social isolation, I had thought of you as the last woman I would have met to feel the greatest and the most precious emotions in life before dying. You neither recognized nor respected my love for you and this harsh refusal prevented me completely from being myself, a man in love.

Soon after I learned that because of your past experiences, you were very bitter with all your exes. Therefore, you struggled with a heavy depression that forced you to take antidepressants for years and hide yourself with the curtains closed and the shutters half lowered. Then I remembered our discussion three years earlier in Florence in the conversation class with the young Greek and understood why you had expressed such negative feelings towards men. You spent many hours on the mobile every night, maybe looking for a new relationship in order to be able to forget the last one. You usually got up late in the morning instead of going out door knocking in the community and trying to find any available work in the meantime. You had refused to try a couple of positions as a waitress that I had found you in two cafés arguing that the wages wouldn't be decent enough. You didn't want to consider a career change by doing a short training course; thus you had seriously limited your potential to find a different job. It seemed as if the wool factory was the only place where you could work.

Another day we went to Maremagnum center and the Boqueria market in Barcelona and you ridiculed me all day. I attempted to walk away from you, but I suddenly turned around to satisfy a whim with an affectionate kiss. However, I quickly changed my mind because I knew you would misunderstand me.
Later on in a café I decided to put an end to the situation:
«Okay Isabel, I know you don't like me at all.»
«Are you disappointed?»
«Yes of course, but I will have to let you go.»
«Let me go? How do you like these?»
Then you pushed out your chest shaking your boobs.
...
I was dumbfounded and couldn't believe your vulgarity. It was the second time you appeared so openly to be looking for sex. Obviously, I wasn't worthy of your love, but I was good enough for sex. I felt very much offended and it was the right moment to break up with you and leave, but I couldn't because I didn't have the strength yet.

I don't know how many partners you've had, but according to you, you had only once come close to getting married. You two had bought the apartment together, but then you had cancelled the wedding for some reason. One of your recent and painful experiences was over a fifty-five-year-old wealthy lawyer from Barcelona who had suddenly abandoned you after only a month. However, in your words, your sadness wasn't due to the loss of the man you wanted, but rather to the deprivation of the financial security that the lawyer would have guaranteed you.

The next day I went to Barcelona to buy you a birthday present. I didn't know what to give you, but because you were previously looking for a Dolce & Gabbana perfume, I eventually decided for *Velvet Rose*. While still in Barcelona, I remembered all your fake jewelries that you had shown me at home and all of the sudden I decided to give you something that represented a fraction of what you meant to me. I visited many stores and finally headed to *Suarez*, a very elegant jewelry store with a controlled opening door and two armed guards inside who watched my every move. They showed me many beautiful necklaces, including one that I liked right away. I wanted to bring the whole world at your feet, but even though I didn't intend to spend that much, I pictured it around your neck and bought it in a heartbeat.

That afternoon I came to you to give you the perfume as a little thought and I told you that I had bought another present for your birthday. You tried the perfume, but it didn't seem as if you liked it. Then I took your hand and put it on my cheek to feel your caress, but you quickly withdrew it because of the hardness of my unshaven face. Instead, you hugged me for the very first time, delighting my heart and conquering my soul with your sweetness as a spiritual being or a wind that had taken all my senses with it. I smelled the divine fragrance of citrus, lily, moss and roses of every species and felt so much vitality that I wanted to hold you in my arms for eternity. I squeezed you into a warm and solid embrace, trying to express love without saying a word. Moments later as you began to retract yourself, I released you slowly and with much reluctance, then I left.

On the fifth day you invited me to lunch and told me to bring my laundry. You washed it together with yours, but when I tried to help you hang it on the rear balcony, you insisted that I should go watch the football match on tv. I don't like sport and I would have preferred to spend as much time as possible with you, but I reluctantly agreed. I didn't know what you had in mind, but it seemed as if you wanted to stage some kind of daily routine in which your man is sitting in front of the tv with a remote control in one hand and a beer in the other, while you cheerfully do the household chores. I didn't like the way you cooked nor what you ate, maybe because you couldn't afford a better diet. So for our next meeting, I decided to surprise you with my culinary skills and cook for us while sipping Muga Rioja and conversing about life to get to know each other better:

«What's in the bag? Have you done some shopping?»

«Yes, I have brought some fresh ingredients to cook for you.»

«No, you don't have to cook for me.
I am sure you are an excellent cook.»

«But look at this tender piece of meat.»

«What kind of meat is this?
I have never seen meat cut this way.»

«It's beef tenderloin. I was going to cook roast beef with sautéed mushrooms and red wine sauce.»

«No, I think it's better to eat out.»

«Really?»

«Yes, I know a good restaurant in the city.»

You put everything in the fridge and then took me to a pizzeria in the historic center of the city.

The next afternoon you called me on your way back from the supermarket. I left my room and ran in your direction so fast that I hyperventilated. I saw you carrying two heavy shopping bags and you were out of breath. I wanted so much to hug you, but you evaded my attempt. Then you told me we couldn't meet for a couple of days because of a stomach ailment. I carried your bags until the entrance of your building and offered to take care of you, but when you refused, I left you in peace for two days, struggling with myself to decide what to do with you. I was still emotionally too attached to you and decided to stay in Rubí until your birthday, hoping you would change your attitude. In the meantime, I felt fantastic and didn't have any obvious symptoms, probably due to the wonderful weather or rather due to the way I felt being so close to you.

I called you two days later and you invited me to lunch again. I rang your intercom about twenty minutes later and when you opened the entrance of the building, you sent down the elevator. When I reached your level, you were waiting for me at the door. We were both happy to see each other again:
«Hello beautiful, how is your stomach?»
«Hi Elias, it's fine and it has return to normality.»
«I brought you some flowers.»
«It's Sunday, where did you get them?»
«From a stall on *La Rambla*.»
«Did you go all the way to Barcelona just to buy me flowers?»
«Yes, because the florist in the neighborhood was closed and I didn't find anything in the city either.»

«How foolish?» you said laughing at me.
«I also brought you this.»
«What's that? A shopping trolly?»
«Yes, to save you the hassle of carrying heavy shopping bags from the supermarket.»
«But I am not a granny.»
«I know. A shopping trolly doesn't have anything to do with age. This one is compact and very practical for long distances.»
«I don't want it.»
«Okay, give it to someone else.»
A short while later:
«Darling, look here. Your meat has gone bad.»
«Darling?»
«Can we freeze it or do we have to throw it away?»
«Why didn't you eat it?»
«I didn't know what to do with it. Can you take it down?»
You couldn't justify my merriment for being with a hot-blooded Spanish woman, so endearing and sensual with sparkling eyes, a seductive smile, a cascade of golden wavy hair and a cheerful mood for seeing me again. You wore your only beautiful dress, the same elegant blue dress, a gift from the rich lawyer which you had on that day in the hallway of Il David Institute and you spoke my favorite language. Simply love!
You cooked frozen junk food for us again and shortly after lunch you asked me why I didn't burp. I helped you clearing the coffee table in the living room and when I was washing the dishes, you approached the sink to rinse a cloth and laying an arm on mine, you leaned against my left side.

I paused to let you do it and soon after I noticed that our tactile connection was causing me a palpable tingling sensation, or a vigorous and constant current of energy flowing from your body to mine, stimulating all my senses with the kind of delight I had never felt before. Our faces were very close and the temptation to getting just a little closer for a first kiss was growing stronger. But I could not find the courage because I wasn't your type. I wasted the precious moment and when I finished washing the dishes, I moved away and leaned against the kitchen wall with a fake smile to mask my great disappointment:
«Did you enjoy peeking down my dress?»
«Yes, but I enjoyed even more feeling your touch.»
Unable to express myself verbally, I approached you and put my arm on yours to attempt to describe what I meant, but because I couldn't, I returned to my previous spot at the wall.
Then all of a sudden, you approached me in a hurry and leaping at me, you pushed your entire body against mine and both of us against the wall so hard and so tightly that there wasn't even any air between us. *¡Ay caramba!* You took my breath away, but immediately after, feeling an immense euphoria and wearing a satisfying smile from ear to ear, I closed my eyes while smelling the scent of your skin and feeling our hearts beating as one. It was so wonderful that all my senses became overwhelmed by emotions and I died and found the two of us at the gate of the garden of Eden, as if we were about to be let in. Bless my soul! However, this incredible celestial vision didn't last long as a few moments later you suddenly wriggled away from me due to an involuntary reaction of one of my organs. Damn!

Although I really liked what you did, I was deprived of words, because considering all the ice and emotional barriers between us, it was the most lascivious and misplaced act I had ever seen a woman perform. I had tried to point out that the touch was diminishing the emotional distance between us, but you had completely misunderstood me. You had crossed my personal boundary with a vulgar act and had sexually embarrassed me, whereas on other occasions you hadn't even let me touch your hands. Then grabbing a bottle of disinfectant to pour in the sink drain, you almost jokingly hit my groin with it. After that you still kept teasing me, wondering why I was so hypnotized by the vision of a woman in a dress at my age, destroying what little dignity that I had left in me.

You were the essence of your true self and empowered by the elegant dress you wore, acted with confidence and your natural charm. So for me there was no other woman more beautiful or any other feeling more precious. Your manners though, made you extremely different and too far off from the lady you could have been. It seemed as if you constantly thought about sex, whereas I didn't have sexual thoughts at the time and I would've refused to run with you in the bedroom. Not wanting to criticize you, I attempted to practice reverse psychology to provoke your hidden qualities. I thanked you for the hospitality and expressing many respectful compliments, I bowed to you repeatedly. I was hoping my exaggerated courtesy would make you comprehend what I meant and would make you more respectful of yourself, but laughing at me the entire time, you asked me to leave.

The practice is known as *The Michelangelo Phenomenon*, it's an interpersonal process and occurs when partners consciously agree to practice marital therapy by influencing and asserting each other to become their ideal selves and ideal partners. This deliberate idealization is a satisfying benevolence that could over time transform from wishful thinking to reality, just like sculpting a masterpiece that exists within a very rough block of marble. I treated you like a very respectable lady, but it was obvious that you had no respect for me and considered me a laughing stock.

Once in a bar you tried to flirt with me again:
«I really like when men "*kiss me there*" and I would like to tattoo a pair of lips high up on one of my thighs.»
I would have offered you my lips if you had respected me with some recognition, instead of treating me only like a sex toy. So I kept looking at you until you reacted to my silence with two grimaces, that is to say; I was much too serious.
Later on you completely gave up on me:
«When do you return to Dublin?»
«Why? Have I been too boring for you?»
«No, but you have already been here for more than a week.»
«Yes, and it's only a few days left to your birthday.»
«I think it would be better if you left.»
«So you are not going to Paris with me?»
«I don't think so.»
«Okay Isabel, I got it. I will leave as soon as I can.»
From that day forward, you stopped wearing your miniskirt that went up almost to your panties when you drove.

You wanted to get rid of me, but it wasn't a surprise considering our different moral values and principles. We had engaged in extreme opposite roles in which I craved spiritual connections in a woman, while you had only sought out another lover to feel desirable. My impressions of you had changed so drastically that I couldn't wait to leave. By then I was convinced that you weren't looking for a serious story with me and I thought you wanted to return to your thirty-five-year-old ex.

The following evening, my last evening there, we went to the waterfront in Barcelona. About two hours after dinner, you finally agreed to go for a drink in a nice beach bar where I intended to give you your birthday present, but we didn't have much to talk about. I gave you many compliments and thanked you for your hospitality while I was assessing whether or not you deserved the necklace and everything it symbolized for me. I hesitated so long that in the end it was time to return to Rubí. Later on we were sitting in your car in front of my hotel and you remained silent with your head down. I had told you that I loved you more than any other man and you had laughed at me. Nothing I had said or done mattered to you and there was no other way or a better occasion to honor my words and show my love for you, than with something tangible that would make you believe me:
«I have carried your present in my backpack all evening.
It's not your birthday yet and we are not in Paris as I had hoped, but I want to give it to you now.
Here you are! Happy birthday in advance.»
«Thanks!»

Then in the calm of the late night, I noticed a local police patrol approaching us and parking right behind our car and turning off their engine, watching us:
«What a beautiful box, it's so elegantly wrapped.»
«Well?»
«I don't want to open it before my birthday.»
«No? I would very much like to see your reaction.»
«Okay!»
«No, don't shake it.»
«It's a necklace!»
«It could be.»
You unwrapped it very slowly as if you were enjoying it:
«*Madre mía!*»
It took your breath away. Then you froze for quite a while, silently staring at a big lustering white pearl of the South Australian seas, symbolizing purity, innocence, honesty and perfection, set in an elegant cone covered in small diamonds, representing love and prosperity and spreading all their energy in glittering prisms of fire, paired with a sophisticated white gold chain that crossed it as a symbol of inspiration and spirituality.
Moments later you shed a few tears of joy without taking your eyes off the jewel between your fingers:
«Let me put it on you.
It looks very good on you, as if it was custom made for you.»
I was hoping for a tender kiss, but you remained silent and still kept your head down to avoid eye contact. Meanwhile, the police officers started their car when they noticed you were crying and drove next to your window:

«Excuse me ma'am, is everything alright here?»
«Yes thanks» you smiled at him.
«Good night then!»
«Good night officer.
It must have been very expensive.»
«Yes, but you are worth it.
I wanted to thank you for keeping me alive during my illness.»
«Get out of the car.»
«Why?»
«I want to hug you.»
I hugged you for a last time, smelling your hair and playing with your golden waves that reached down the middle of your back. I was once again lost and entered a celestial dimension which deeply nourished all my senses as I whispered in your ear:
«I would die for you.»
«No, everyone has their own life and your life is yours.»
You still didn't want or couldn't acknowledge my love for you.
I stared at you smiling to capture the image of you wearing the necklace which adorned your natural beauty with a Duchenne smile and a sense of contentment:
«Good bye Isabel!»
...
«Good bye? See you later!» you said before leaving.
I was alive because of you and I had already repaid your gift of life with my respect and gratitude. On the morning of my tenth day in Spain and just two days short of your birthday, I returned to Dublin trying to forget you.

A change of heart

I thought about you on your birthday when we could have been together in Paris, but we weren't even friends.
One of the following days you called me:
«Isabel? What a pleasant surprise.»
«Hi Elias, how are you?»
«I am okay. Did you call me by mistake?»
«No, I wanted to tell you something.»
«Yes, what is it?»
«I have decided to come and visit Dublin.»
...
«Interesting! When do you want to come?»
«What do you say about next week? Are you busy?»
«Yes, but I can take a few days off.
Okay, give me a few hours to book you a flight.»
«I can buy the ticket myself.»
«Yes, I know, but you are unemployed.
I will email you the details very soon.»
«Okay thanks a lot, we talk later.»
I didn't know what to think, I wanted to believe you were coming for me. But why? Had I suddenly become your type?
Had you started to develop feelings for me?
Maybe I had given you the wrong impression by offering you a very expensive necklace and you thought I was rich. In any case, I booked you a one-way flight the same day and decided not to talk about us and not to ask you why you had come to me until you ran into my arms.

The day of your arrival I rented a car and went to the airport. I meant to buy you some flowers, but I didn't find anything good. When you arrived, you were wearing the necklace, but hugging each other, I didn't smell any perfume. Then I took you directly to Malahide near Dublin and after a couple of drinks in a pub, we visited the castle and took some pictures of you. After that we went for a long stroll in Howth marina and for dinner, I took you to a French restaurant. You had earlier asked for a separate bedroom and I had prepared the master bedroom in my rented apartment. Then you presented your souvenirs, including two books of Spanish grammar, but I didn't understand the reason. You knew I loved Italian more than any other language, yet it seemed as if you wanted to encourage me to learn your idiom.

That night we went to bed around three am. You were sitting on the inside of a two-seater sofa and I was on a three-seater next to you. You confided in me and told me that you still could and very much wished to become a mother. You also mentioned your deep sorrow over your inability to understand why the rich lawyer had suddenly abandoned you despite the great sex. I expressed empathy for your pain, but I wasn't sure if you needed a few pats on the hand, an arm around your shoulders or a hug. I knew about the power of physical contact, yet I didn't want to touch you in a weak moment. It was the very first time you had spoken about your feelings and it was a good sign of your trust in me. I was looking forward for more, but as it turned out, this was the only time you opened your heart to me, maybe because you didn't get the support you were looking for.

The next morning we loaded the car, set the most direct route to western Ireland and a few hours later we stopped at a roadside café. After lunch I opened the car door for you and once you put on the seat belt, you kept looking at me with a jovial smile. I stared at you for a while and wanted so much to lean inside and kiss you, but I hesitated too long and soon that beautiful moment vanished. We were both happy and then I surprised you with an exquisite chocolate box that I had previously hidden in the car. You started to unwrap one chocolate at a time and rubbing it deliciously all around my lips, you were trying to put it in my mouth, while I turning my head and looking over my shoulders, was trying to reverse and exit the parking spot.

What a great sensation! Seeing you happy, feeling your delicate fingers on my lips and then indulging in the sophisticated taste of the chocolate that quickly melted in the mouth. I couldn't help but grabbing your hand every time and kissing your fingers repeatedly which tasted sweeter than the chocolates. Meanwhile a lady who watched us as she was walking through the parking, cheerfully shouted: «That's love!»
But when I smiled at you in affirmation for the lady's comment, you instantly stopped putting chocolates in my mouth, ruining those lovely moments and repeatedly denying your affectionate gestures. It was disappointing, but there was no reason to talk about it. You acted as if you belonged to another, or as if I was made of stone and shouldn't feel anything for your sweetness. Later on when I tried to capture your charm and beauty with my phone, you wouldn't let me.

In Galway city in county Clare, you asked me to find a B&B room with two beds. Then we went to the picturesque cliffs of Moher that extend for 8 kilometers with panoramic views of stunning landscapes overlooking the Aran Islands and the Atlantic. There, you refused to be photographed, but took a picture of me in a hurry. Later on during the sunset with dark clouds yet gloriously serene and dreamy, I was feeling so exhilarated with euphoria that when the sun had finally sunk into the ocean, I wanted to eternally seal the moment with a first kiss. But when you turned around and realized that I was slowly approaching your face, you promptly turned away your head with an annoyed expression:
«Were you about to kiss me?»
And I walked a couple of steps away in my disappointment.

On the second day we continued towards Castlebar in county Mayo and for lunch we found a bistro in a village where we were the only customers. Having ordered food, I went to the bathroom and walked out with wet hands. When I got back to our table, you started to complain as if you hated everything I did:
«Why haven't you dried your hands?»
«Because the paper towels were finished.»
«Why didn't you use the hand dryer?»
«There was none.»
«Couldn't you use some toilet paper?»
«Yes, I suppose, but I didn't enter the toilet.»
«Why not?»
«Because I didn't want to touch anything.»
«But how could you leave the bathroom like this?»

«I am sorry Isabel. Please don't get upset.
Look, I am drying my hands with the napkin.»
«That's not the right way.»
«Yes, I know. I said I am sorry.»
«I don't appreciate it at all.»
«For God's sake! Please don't think about it anymore.
Look where we are, let's talk about something else.»
I was hoping for a romantic getaway for us, but things started to go very wrong from our third day on the road and I was shocked to discover your personality. In the B&B in Castlebar I wanted to shave and decided to use a small basin near the entrance in the main room and leave the bathroom free. Then digging in my vanity case, I showed you a small cute bottle of essential oil that I had bought to massage your body:
«What is it?»
«It's the essence of lavender diluted in sweet almond oil.»
You took the bottle and opened it to smell it:
«Hmm, smells nice!»
«Yes, doesn't it?» I replied smiling at you.
Then I wet my face with water and accidentally splashed some droplets around the basin. When you saw that on the floor, you complained and I apologizing, wiped the tiles. I kept my chest pushed out and held in my belly as much as I could, because you for some reason were walking around behind me, so we could stare and smile at each other in the mirror. I shaved twice and then I went to take a long shower. That evening I had a lot of confidence because of the way you were paying attention to me and I thought you were going to bewitch me.

Later on you were laying down on my bed and connected to the B&B Wi-Fi, watched music videos on your mobile. I approached you and kneeling on the moquette, I tilted a little towards you to see your screen when all of a sudden:
«You are too close to my body» you said with indignation.
«What?»
Yes, I had tried to impress you with my body when I was shaving and I admit I was hoping for a little goodnight kiss, but nothing more. Your protest offended me because I couldn't understand the reason for such comment from a woman who had previously tried to seduce me in every way:
«I wanted to be near you just to watch the videos.
I don't understand why you have come to me if you don't like to spend time with me?»
«I've already told you; you are not my type and I don't think I can ever feel anything for you. I came to Ireland only as a friend and you shouldn't have any other expectations from me.
Do you understand?»
I remained silent when I felt your words had cut my heart in two halves. You were in a good mood, but something had happened while I was taking the shower and it had affected you so much that you had to express hostility and resentment. It was a hard blow to discover that not only you hadn't come for me, but you didn't even like me as a friend. Then you moved to your bed in the little open attachment to the main room to continue playing with your precious phone and most probably chat with your ex in Spain. Meanwhile, I was sinking further into an acute state of depression for the first time in my life.

You didn't behave like a friend, but like an extremely arrogant and immature teenager, demonstrating your most ignoble and damaging qualities without noticing my emotional breakdown. It soon became even more painful to endure your lack of empathy for my obvious suffering. You reacted as if I had made a sexual advance towards you or as if I had betrayed your trust, so you felt entitled to ignore me as punishment. I looked at you a couple of times in search of support, but you were very busy with your phone. Soon after we went to bed without saying a word to each other, but I went through hell during the agonizing hours of that night and deleted every photo I had of you in my mobile and my PC while you slept peacefully.

The next morning, I couldn't eat breakfast. Then in that beautiful riverside market blocked by anguish, I wasn't even able to talk, so much so that I finally burst into tears. In the meantime, you were only worried about keeping a certain distance from me instead of intervening trying to comfort me. You behaved like a block of ice and showed that not only you weren't a caring and loving woman, but a very cold-hearted and selfish person. You reacted like a victim, as if I was deliberately ruining your vacation with such nonsense as imposing my love on to you. You made me feel so embarrassed that I had to apologize to you repeatedly for not being a merry company, but you still kept ignoring me. You treated me like a butler and yet you didn't seem to enjoy or appreciate anything I did for you. During lunch you became very quiet and I didn't know if you were still angry with me or if you had argued with your cx online:

«What is wrong Isabel?»
«I don't care what you do for me.»
«No? Why not?»
«Because I have built a wall around me to protect myself.»
You said casting your contemptuous glances at me.
I thought you were willing to give me a fair chance; instead you treated me like an idiot. I felt disgusted by your attitude and there was nothing more to say, so I asked:
«Then what are we doing here together?»
I was furious because not even this silly excuse justified your unparalleled arrogance. You too were full of rage and seemed angrier with me because I didn't understand your reason:
«You have created a mess, Isabel.
I think we should separate here and go our different ways.»
«Fine!»
I sighed and looked away thinking:
«We are in a remote area of Ireland. I can't leave you here with little money and an inadequate English. What do you think about continuing the journey until we return to Dublin?»
«Okay.»
I was traveling with an immature woman who was struggling with loneliness, depression, unemployment and who was very bitter with all her exes. A very confused woman with nostalgia for her last ex, who had come to travel with another man in love with her, while considering returning to her ex. A desolate and desperate woman who was presumably longing for love, and yet she had willfully built an impenetrable fortress around herself to protect herself from love.

You had kicked me out of your life in Spain for refusing to treat the woman I loved as a sexual object. Then you had the audacity to come to me only thanks to the necklace, to deliberately take advantage of my emotional weakness while trying to solve your problems with the ex in Spain. Later on you had started scolding me for small and insignificant issues beyond my control, forcing me to apologize to you and yet you wouldn't let it be. It seemed as if not only you lacked emotional maturity, wisdom and life experience for your age, but also the right approach and attitude for love. So everything that I had realistically thought you were, turned out to be very wrong. Thus my feelings for you reluctantly started to diminish and you slowly began to die in me, because I couldn't find any admirable characteristic in your personality.

A confidant

When we were on the way to Sligo, you asked me:
«What are you going to do once established in Italy?»
«Well, I lost almost everything I had during the last three years, but I still can rent a big and beautiful country house and convert it into an elegant and cozy B&B.»
«Why not one in a city?»
«Because I love the countryside and I know many people would appreciate a nice and quiet place with clean air.»
«I like your idea very much and I could join you to realize this dream together.»
It would have been an ideal union, but I couldn't reply to you considering our relationship and your attitude towards work and you didn't make any further comments.

That evening in Sligo I was very dispirited and although hungry, I didn't want to eat. You weren't hungry because at lunch you always ate too much in order not to waste food, but you insisted I should eat something. We went out and found a nice restaurant where we drank some good wine while waiting for the takeaway pizza that I had ordered and I couldn't believe the unprecedented kindness and attention you had shown me. Your thoughtfulness had significantly reduced the emotional distance between us and had made us connect as friends. I wasn't sure, maybe this was what you were trying to tell me: *"This is who I really am"*.

I ate a few bites of the pizza in the B&B and then chose an online movie, *The Outsider,* which I had seen before. The story takes place in a remote Amish community, where a wounded gunman becomes attracted to a beautiful widower who initially resists his humble ways, until one day she goes to him and taking him by the hand, surrenders to love. I chose this movie to show you a certain similarity to my attitude towards you, but I doubted you had realized it. You were aware of my affection for you and it was your turn to show if you felt anything for me. In the morning while I was waiting for you to get up, I wanted to sing along with Andrea Bocelli, *Time to say goodbye*, but then I decided to play *Sometimes when it rains*, by Secret Garden to stimulate your emotional capacity, but you didn't show any reaction.

In Donegal city we visited the castle and, in the evening, we went to a pub to listen to live Irish music. Then the other tourists kept staring at you because you refused to join me near the stage. Soon you became hysterical by the attention and forced us to leave quickly. Your abrupt outburst of social anxiety didn't even stop outside despite my repeated apologies. You crouched on the sidewalk and refused to walk with me, blaming me for taking you to a crowded pub. Trying to distract you, I tempted you with dinner at *The Harbour*, a very popular restaurant. There, while I was translating the English menu for you, you felt embarrassed when the couple next to our table looked at us once hearing Italian and you became angry with me again. I had to apologize to you repeatedly and lower my voice almost to the level of a whisper to keep you happy.

Then when we returned to that gorgeous B&B, you went straight on your bed with your back against the wall and as usual started to watch music videos on the mobile instead of spending time with me. I really wanted us to do something together, but ended up kneeling on the carpet next to you and didn't spend much time in that position before complaining about my sore knees. You, taking your eyes off the phone, slowly turned your head to the empty place next to you on the bed and then back on the phone again in total silence, as if to sarcastically suggest:
"Why don't you come up on the bed next to me?"
It would have been a nice gesture if you had looked at me and asked me, instead you refused to offer me even that little comfort so as not to reveal any weakness in caring for me. You displayed yet another undesirable characteristic that made you even more unsuitable for a loving and caring relationship. My instinctive and natural reaction was to withdraw, because I could not feel any closeness in your presence. I could not even watch anything online because I hadn't brought the headset. So I started to play Solitaire on my laptop while you were listening to your music. We were both in the same room, but we were both all alone, because you didn't want to have anything to do with me, except when you were hungry or wanted something.

The more I got to know you, the more disappointed I became and I couldn't understand why you had brought with you the emotional baggage of your last relationship. I did not like your vulgar language and how you casually mentioned sexual organs or when you made the movement of love making.

I had huge difficulty believing that you had deliberately started a sexual relationship with the best friend of one of your exes for revenge, so much so that you had eventually broken up their longtime friendship. I didn't want to know that you went with any man, no matter younger, older or even married, just to satisfy your insatiable sexual appetite. I couldn't stop imagining you in various positions in that bed with all those men, who according to you sniffed your panties even after sex. How very disgusting! These types of confessions were the kind of dirty pillow talk you could have shared with a one-night stand guy and not with a man who had feelings for you. In my opinion, there is no benefit in sharing this topic with anyone at all.

I didn't want to hear stories about your sexual partners and nothing honorable that you had done for love. But you were so smug and talked about these sexual adventures with so much pride as if they were the greatest accomplishments of your life. I couldn't understand the reason for your exhibitionism, for having publicly shown your breasts and having been fined for indecent exposure and for going to nudist beaches in Barcelona. Despite an open mind and a non-moralistic attitude, I reluctantly began to question your ethics and principles, wondering what kind of woman you were. I began to think of you as a ruthless man-eater or an immoral sexual predator who wouldn't hesitate to even break up a marriage to get what you wanted. These were the kind of impressions you gave me and made me think the worst of you, because you weren't acting according to your age or like a respectable lady.

The next morning you wanted to take a shower, but moments later ran out lightly covered and took my breath away. I watched you digging as a left-hander in your suitcase on the table, while with the other hand, you held a small towel whose upper corners barely met around your waist. I looked at the golden waves of your hair flowing along your smooth back and the silky skin of your shoulders, I stared at your bra and examining your curvy and slender waist, I tried very hard to focus on the most hidden part of your body that to me seemed naked through the inverted V-opening made by the towel. Then I followed your voluptuous thighs all the way down your long legs, after which I moved my eyes back on the darkened central area in silence and without blinking. So before you ran back to the bathroom, I had already registered the most seductive view of your body in my mind and I liked everything so much that I was dying to touch you.

I don't know why you hadn't cover yourself with the big towel and I was so focused on looking at your body that I didn't realize what you had taken with you to the bathroom. Maybe it was a deliberate act to arouse excitement in me, but considering your lack of interest in spending time with me, it wasn't likely at all. The clear glass shower box was right in front of the bathroom door which closed with a latch. I had hung a sock on the door handle to cover the keyhole when I was showering. I wasn't sure if you were aware of it, so I thought of watching your body through the keyhole while you were showering. But then again, I managed to resist the temptation; I still had enough respect for you not to violate your privacy.

The next day we went to the Slieve League cliffs in the heart of Donegal which are less steep than the cliffs of Moher, but about four times higher. There, you ignored me again as if you were alone. I once saw you attempting to approach a few sheep that were grazing on a steep terrain and trying to chase them as they strayed from you. Only later did you explain to me that you loved the smell of sheep and wanted to sniff them to bring back good memories of when you worked in the wool factory.

Then exploring in the area, we reached a small fishing port at Teelin Pier, the most romantic place we had seen until then. The fishermen had gone away a long time ago and we were all alone. We walked to the water edge, watching the small and colorful fishing boats with encrusted hulls, the fishing nets, the rolled ropes, the crab traps and the splashes of large fish playing near the surface of the water as we listened to the shrill verse of the seagulls gliding on the sea breeze above us. It was a beautiful afternoon and moments later we were leaning on a short wall overlooking the port, where some boats were moored, but we had nothing to say to each other. Hoping you would kiss me this time, I approached you and stayed so close that our upper arms were touching. Then I looked at your profile in anticipation, but you didn't look back at me. You were very quiet and thoughtful, as if you were missing someone else by your side and having refused to kiss me previously, I didn't know what else to do. We were standing there in total silence for a while as if each one of us was all alone and another one of those magical moments that comes only once in a life time, vanished again, forever.

We had time to explore only a small part of the Emerald Isle, which is the poetic name for Ireland thanks to its very lush and green countryside. We were very lucky because it wasn't cold and didn't rain at all while we were on the road. The weather was wonderful and allowed us to enjoy breathtaking views of many rivers, tranquil lakes and natural wonders either with a grey sky or the occasional sunshine and the beautiful cotton clouds. I had not taken any medication since my return from Australia, but incredibly I was still in good health without any symptoms and unusually for the season, I didn't even have a common cold. I wanted to believe that I had finally survived the infection and that I could look forward to an almost normal life, but I had to wait until the winter to make sure.

The impasse

We still didn't have any emotional bond and maybe that is why it had become very difficult to relate to each other from Belfast onwards. Your headset didn't work, so you put a lot of pressure on me expecting me to simultaneously translate the comments on the sightseeing tour of the city into my limited Italian. I just wanted to run away from you. Back in the hotel room, while we were standing and talking about something, you opened the zipper of your trousers and pushed away the flaps. I didn't react until moments later when you put your hand on your tummy and started slowly moving it downwards. I was standing by your side and couldn't see much, but because I didn't like it:

«What are you doing Isabel?»

«Sorry!» you said and ran into the bathroom.

I don't know if it was involuntary or not, but I didn't expect such provocative act from a friend. Then I remembered that we had different mentalities and maybe this was your way of trying to seduce me without arousing the idea of doing it intentionally. If so, I couldn't help wondering what could have changed since the night in Castlebar when you complained about me being too close to your body. Maybe you had argued with the ex for having come to me and you didn't want him to decide for you. Perhaps you saw me as a substitute to fill the void left by him or you simply enjoyed traveling with me, but you missed sex. Whatever the reason was, I didn't think you wanted me for who I was.

We had pushed the two single beds together to have more space on either side of the beds. Later on wearing your pajamas, you were sitting on your half taking off your knee socks. I was sitting on the other half of the bed while various sensual and passionate scenarios with you were invading my mind. I imagined lowering the light, playing Zen music and rubbing the massage oil all over your body. I slowly stretched my arm with a smile and kept my hand close to one of your bare legs as if I couldn't quite reach it while we stared at each other. I was hoping you would smile at me or move your leg to touch my hand as a sign of consent, but you put on a very serious and defensive face, as if to say:
"Don't you dare touch me".
When I realized you weren't interested, I pulled back my arm.

My mind was already intoxicated with desire, so later on while I was taking a shower, I wished you were with me. But it wasn't a realistic desire, because except for the quick hug at the airport and for kissing your fingers when you were putting chocolates in my mouth, I don't remember us touching each other again, not even accidentally. When I got out of the shower, I found only a hand towel in the bathroom and I soon remembered having seen the big one on top of the nightstand. I had to ask you to bring it to me and I was hoping you wouldn't think I had done it on purpose. I put the little towel around me, completely covering the front and then pushed out my chest and pulled in my belly as much as I could. When I opened the bathroom door to take the big towel, you smiled at me and hesitated for an instant while looking at my chest.

Later on without a strong Wi-Fi signal and nothing good on tv, I had stretched out on my side of the bed, staring at the ceiling. Then you suddenly approached me on your knees on the bed and bending over my head, you were looking into my eyes with an unappealing expression devoid of any sensuality to tempt me with your imposing natural assets as if you were demanding:
"Take me!"
Blimey! You had just rejected my attempt and now this?
Your body looked extremely tempting and I liked having almost everything in my face. You had become more daring, trying to take control and conquer me with your ridiculous manipulations without knowing enough about my psychology. Although I really desired you, as an emotionally very evolved man, I had to resist you because you didn't act in a natural way and I knew you were not doing it specifically for me. So I quoted you:
«You are too close to my body.»
Then I turned my head to the other side to distract myself before losing control. Next, I put my hands on my tommy and started twiddling my thumbs, making you realize that I would rather get bored to death than touching you. Because I couldn't trust you, I decided to protect my love from your degrading sexual needs. Then you quickly retreated crawling away on all four. Although we both desired each other very much, the situation was totally stalled simply because our motivations were so different. You fooled yourself pretending not to be interested in me and at the same time you were trying to make me touch you, while I wanted to show that you were not irresistible, but above all, that I didn't like your devious ways. What a mess!

Soon after we had gone to bed to sleep:
«There is a cold breeze from the window» you said.
«Well it's on your side of the bed, close it.»
«Can you do it?»
I put on my trousers under the duvet and then I got up:
«Couldn't you get up without the trousers?»
«No!»
I replied and after shutting the window, I returned to bed taking off my trousers, again under the duvet. I couldn't understand why you wouldn't make a start with a compliment or a goodnight kiss instead of constantly trying to manipulate me. That night we practically slept in the same bed despite the sexual tension that had accompanied us throughout the entire evening.

During a break on the way back to Dublin, you again asked me for advice on how to fight negative thoughts. But when I was talking, you decided to correct my confusion for; *"Come così!"* instead of just, *"Così!"*, (like this). You were very sweet and kept making fun of me in a pleasant way. But I wasn't listening to a word you were saying. I was lost trying to decide whether or not catch you off guard, grabbing your face and kissing your lips as passionately as I could and then finish saying:
"Così?"
Although I knew the kiss would have felt absolutely wonderful, I hesitated way too long simply because my perception of you, wouldn't let me. It didn't seem appropriate kissing a woman with such peculiar behavior and so many dark clouds about you that were still hovering on my mind.

In Dublin instead of asking you to leave, I introduced you to my brother and showed you his restaurants within a minute from each other. The next morning we went to the Garden of Ireland, to the Wicklow Mountains National Park. The jewel of this region is Glendalough, *"The valley of the two lakes"*. It is a monastic settlement dating back to the 6th century with the cross of St. Kevin, the founder and the first abbot, the ruins of six churches, a circular stone tower and an ancient cemetery with tombstones and Celtic crosses covered in moss. But you did not appreciate the beauty or history of that place and failed to notice how some tombstones with the passage of time had leaned on the adjacent ones, as if the deceased relied on their loved ones even in death:
«Is something wrong Isabel?»
«Why have you brought me here?»
«This place is one of the most historic sites of Ireland.»
«No, it's a cemetery and the dead should be left alone.»
Then you started to walk away in protest.
Later on I enjoyed the walk to the upper lake during which I as a play, started to softly push you off the trail on the lawn. It was a pleasant surprise to see you doing the same with me smiling as if it was a spontaneous and beautiful manifestation of love. My mind was messed up again and I didn't dare to believe you liked me, it could not be so. If that was the case, why on all the other occasions you acted as if you couldn't care less about me? I felt frustrated and could not understand your mood and your contradictory messages, because nothing you did made sense. I was also very much in conflict with my prejudices about your ways of dealing with men.

Although I was about to return to Italy, I was willing to stay in Ireland for as long as it took for you to get back on your feet. I wanted you to rediscover your natural joy and happiness making new friends and learning English in a school that I had shown you and then give you a job with good salary. I had also offered you my heart and I was convinced that love would've overcome all our flaws. But you had rejected everything and had instead chosen to continue living in the past because you didn't want to surrender to me. Perhaps the temptation to return to the mighty arms of your thirty-five-year-old ex was much stronger than all my love, all my life experience and resourcefulness.

I knew that it takes time for love to flourish and that love is shown not only with words, but also with various gestures. But there had been too many times during which you had behaved very badly and repeatedly pushed me too far away from you. You had further weakened my self-esteem and cut my wings from the beginning in Spain. Then in Ireland, I had not yet been able to find out your real reason for coming to me. Basically, I had not been able to understand or change anything in this confused relationship where I couldn't be myself without your sincerity. We still had time to talk, but as a repeatedly rejected man, I certainly didn't have any reason to initiate a conversation about your feelings for me. I couldn't quite figure out what you wanted and I was convinced you could not unlock your heart. I didn't believe you would ever be able to admit what you felt for me, while you were expecting me to love you unconditionally, regardless of your repellent ways.

One day we visited Dublin Castle and later on as we walked to a restaurant, we saw a young girl on the cobbled alleys of Temple Bar, one of Dublin's most charming district for nightly fun:
«Mamma mia, what a gorgeous girl!» you noted.
When she passed us, you turned around checking her behind:
«And look at that sexy body.
Why don't you make a comment?» you asked in amazement.
«Because I am not that kind of man.»
«Didn't you like looking at her?»
«Yes, I did for as long as she was in my field of view.»
Then you mentioned her again even during lunch:
«I don't understand why you didn't react for that girl.»
«That's enough Isabel! I have already told you I am not that kind of man. I don't like to comment, whistle or drool for women.»

Later on, after a stroll in St. Stephen's Green with its shaded boulevards, flower beds and the pond with swans and various ducks and geese, we were headed for the Guinness brewery:
«Oh how nice, I would like very much to see more of Dublin in a horse-drawn carriage.»
«Okay! We can do it another day.»
«But we don't have time.»
«Why not? Are you in a hurry to return to Spain?»
«No, but I am running out of my antidepressant pills.»
I thought you would've felt happy if I had showed you some affection. Hence, I decided to encourage you to stay a few days longer to give us more time to bond and perhaps motivate you to end your dependance on happiness pills:

«Isabel, why don't you stay with me a few more days, trying to give up the pills all together?»
«No, I can't do it. I don't feel good because for the last two days I have taken only half the normal dose.»
«I can try to cheer you up.»
«No thanks, I couldn't absolutely do without the pills.»

The last three days were the most terrible, we had bad weather and you were very annoyed like an unruly child who behaved in a petulant manner and constantly irritated me for no apparent reason. I considered you an emotional burden while you felt rejected and tried to get my attention in the worst possible way. I didn't understand how you could expect me to show you the same affection, considering the way you had treated me in Spain or relying solely on your willingness to have sex with me as you used to do with any man just for fun. Of course the sexual union was very important also to me, but in this very unique case, my strong desire for emotional union had taken the upper hand, because I was looking for a graceful love and I wanted it all or nothing. Given that you had come to me only after receiving an exquisite gift, did not tell me anything about your feelings. I needed you to be truthful and confide in me, because only honesty and sincerity create trust and intimacy. I think your short comings were tied to your useless pride that kept you trapped in you. Furthermore, because of your insecurities, you were forced to keep pretending, perhaps without realizing it or without recognizing that a little humbleness would make you follow your heart and set you free emotionally.

I remember you looking at me with saddened expressions as we once walked under a drizzle and you wondered why I didn't want to share your umbrella with you. In another occasion when we were headed to the botanical garden, you just kept complaining about a possible rain, ruining our happy mood and creating an unpleasant atmosphere between us. I wanted to talk to you and take you by the hand in every occasion, but I couldn't read your mind or put up with your bad temper.
You often asked me:
«Are you really looking for a woman?»
«Yes, but not just any.»
I always answered you to give you clues about your behavior, but this time you didn't want to know my feelings for you and you never asked me what kind of woman I liked.

You are attractive, but you didn't radiate the true beauty that emanate those who possess serenity and inner peace. I could see your unhappiness, but I could neither understand you nor tolerate you. I was so demoralized that I didn't want to be with you, because you acted as if you were immune to me and denied us a beautiful love story. Due to my temporary life in Dublin, I didn't have a tv and because of your undesirable behavior, I was never in the mood to go out with you in the evenings. You had ignored me every night while we were travelling, simply because you preferred the phone which you would connect to the B&B Wi-Fi. But in Dublin you were bored without Internet, because you had forgotten to switch the mobile to data roaming before leaving Spain and you expected me to entertain you.

Another day we visited Kilmainham museum prison in Dublin and then waiting for a taxi, you asked me in English:
«Do you hate me?»
«Yes, you managed to turn love into hatred.»
I didn't mean it and I just said it to provoke a dialogue. But you showed no reaction at all because you wanted to appear strong and perhaps at the same time resented me for not noticing how torn and broken you were.

The tide from high had changed to low and had altered our impressions of each other. You had felt my feelings for you waning and had realized something had gone wrong, but you weren't able to justify it as a result of your behavior. My reluctant apprehension made it difficult for you to reach me and I was looking for additional reasons to give up on you. But it was a weak detachment and it would have been enough if you confided in me or gave me some compliments to rekindle all my cravings. Two days before you left, you suddenly put your arm around my arm in the Powerscourt House and in doing so, you had once again reduced our emotional distance and managed to make me feel wanted for a moment. I did not expect such a cute gesture from a woman who had insulted my integrity, yet I wanted to trap you in my arms and make you mine with a kiss. Instead I became upset and pulled off my arm from yours because by then it was much too late. I was expecting a reaction to start criticizing you, but you managed to keep your composure as if it didn't matter to you. I was disappointed again and later on I still had tears in my eyes during another silent lunch.

During our last evening in the city while you kept complaining, you made a very unexpected comment as we were crossing the river Liffey on the iconic Ha'penny pedestrian bridge:
«And you want us to become a couple.»
«Never!» I cried out spontaneously without really meaning it.
«Don't get angry with me» you yelled at me.
«I am not angry with you» I shouted at you.
I was shocked to hear your comment just as you didn't expect such a response from me. Then a few moments after crossing the river, I saw you collapsing emotionally and having to sit on the window sill of a shop as if you had just discovered the most devastating news of your life. I was very surprised to see your reaction, so I joined you and it took me a while to reflect on what we had just said to each other. We were both sitting there in total silence, stunned and consumed by each other's comments. Soon after you got yourself together, we began to walk against a river of pedestrians who came towards us from the opposite direction without exchanging a word. I thought about taking you to a nearby pub to engage in a dialog, but I was too baffled to talk about anything. I was trying to figure out how you could expect me to be interested in a woman who just couldn't stop playing and pretending. How could you think of us as a couple when you had repeatedly ridiculed my love for you and rejected me for not being your type? Why were you able to see us together now that many things had already gone very wrong and so many precious moments had already been lost forever? I was sure you didn't even want me as a friend, while you thought I still considered you as a partner.

Believing that you were walking next to me, after a few steps I looked over my shoulder to see how you were, but to my horror you were not there. I looked around and saw you at a distance behind me in the middle of the crowded footpath, like a rock protruding out in a stream. You were looking at me from afar and seemed like a lost and frightened little girl with hanging shoulders and a sad face. I knew you had to be suffering deeply, but unfortunately, I wasn't able to comfort you because I too was emotionally torn. I walked to you with an annoyed expression to encourage you to follow me, but I really should have hugged you. Then we headed for the bus stop when we could have taken a taxi and soon after it started pouring. You kept staring at me and touching my cap, you were worried that I could get soaked. I on the other hand, refused to even look at you or share your umbrella with you at the stop during the time it took for the bus to arrive. I don't know how you were feeling, I was feeling furious and outrageous for being this close to you. I loved you so much that I resented you for having messed us up this brutally. There were no vacant double seats available on the upper deck of the bus, so you sat on a seat in front of me and therefore we did not exchange a word on the way back either.

The great pretender

Back in my brother's Italian restaurant we went to my office, but you were still desolate and started to play these songs on my laptop; *Solamente tú*, by Pablo Alborán, *Perdoname*, by Pablo Alborán and Carminho, *Vencer al amor,* by India Martínez, as if you were trying to tell me something without actually using your own words. That's why I also decided to play the songs; *Magari*, by Renato Zero and *Arriverà*, by Modà and Emma to encourage you to confide in me or ask me what you wanted to know, but you showed no other reaction except an intense anguish.

It seemed as if you were trying to encourage me to confide in you first because obviously you didn't have anything to share with me. You too were emotionally exhausted with symptoms of anxiety and the dread for facing the moment of our truth. I got up and sliding your chair towards me to face you, I intended to show empathy by taking your face in my hands and telling you everything with a kiss. Instead I put only the outer edges of my hands around your face because I still felt so irritated that I did not really want to touch you. It wasn't a heartly gesture, however you still waited a few moments until your face became distorted with anger and moving your head rapidly from side to side, you shook away my hands because of my hesitation. Afterwards I withdrew and sat on the floor staring at you in frustration, as I just couldn't deceive you for pity.

I had pointed out to you many times before that it seemed as if you couldn't care less about me and every time you had nothing to say, as if who remains silent, agrees:
«I don't understand why you behave so…resentfully.
It seems to me that I still don't mean anything to you, right?»
It was the turning point for you if you wanted to convince me that I was wrong. I was hoping you would reach out to me, smile at me or tell me anything. I waited for quite a while, but as usual you kept staring at me as if you were demanding an explanation from me instead. You must have been completely discouraged by my comment in the city and it no longer made sense talking about us, let alone admitting your feelings for me:
«Don't you want to answer?»
…
You had reached the breaking point, but apparently fighting the battle of the sexes, there was no chance that you could admit such a shameful weakness in caring for me and had to reject me for the last time. Judging by your history, it is also possible that your sexism over time may have developed into *Misandry,* into hatred for men. It didn't seem as if you could feel any emotions, maybe because your emotional development for some reason had stagnated since your childhood. Hence you behaved like an eternal teenager who had never grown up and therefore didn't have the right mental age. However, it was more plausible that you had difficulty expressing your feelings and perhaps blocked them for fear of getting hurt. Whatever the reason, you preferred to suffer doing what your head dictated to you, instead of relying on your feelings and listening to your heart.

After dinner and the short walk home, I took your scarf in the living room to hang it on the coat rack behind the front door in the hall. But before I did it, I put it on my face smelling the scent of your skin. Then when I hung it up and turned around, I saw you behind my back looking at me, as if to say:
"I am right here."
I would have smiled at you and hugged you if you had shown any other reaction but a miserable face. Instead we just looked at each other and then I walked around you as if you were an obstacle. You behaved too passively, just like a lifeless doll who doesn't speak or smile, doesn't show any emotions, so it feels nothing and doesn't reveal anything about itself. Therefore you weren't responsive or reliable and because you were indifferent, you were always willing to start superficial relationships with any man just to have someone next to you.
Soon after you called me to your room:
«My mobile doesn't charge.»
«Let me see. There is nothing wrong with the phone.»
«So it's working?»
«Yes, as you can see it's charging.»
You were very bored, but you didn't want to come to me, instead you had found such a silly excuse to make me come to you. I realized you wanted us to be together and I would have gladly stayed with you, if you hadn't used such a manipulative strategy. I was not too demanding, I expected you to ask me with a few words. Not wanting to recognize your childish effort, I walked out immediately and left you there alone and annoyed, because you still couldn't stop playing games with me.

For our last supper, we went to my brother's Indian restaurant and at the end of the evening at home:
«Do you have a T-shirt for me to wear in bed?»
«Yes of course. Why?»
«I don't want to wear my newly washed bedclothes for my last night here.»
«Okay!»
I brought you a T-shirt and returned to my bedroom:
«Elias!»
«Yes, what is it?»
«Can you also bring me a pair of shorts?»
I gave you my swimming shorts and then my eyes fell on your breasts, gazing at one of your nipples that was protruding from my T-shirt as you looked at me. Then I returned to my bed when a few moments later you knocked on my door:
«Yes?»
You opened the door and turned on the light:
«I just want to show you how beautiful I am in your clothes.»
You said with a warm and charming smile that any other man would have appreciated, but it meant nothing to me:
«Oh yeah very nice!» I told you without even taking a good look at you or seeing your reaction before you turned off the light and closed the door behind you. I ruined it, I ruined everything I had ever wanted and deprived us from the last opportunity to bond. I ignored your last attempt to involve me, because even though it seemed like a very sweet and romantic gesture, it felt like a heartless move made just to seduce me.
I still didn't know the reason why.

You had shown courage with yet another gesture of love, except that it wasn't a bold move by a confident woman, but a desperate measure by a person without communication skills. We didn't have any bond and lacked intimacy which too often is confused with sex. You had once again preferred the pleasure of physical intimacy which in our case wouldn't have been making love, but just having sex. It seemed like another one of your manipulative strategies aimed at making us fall in love with each other in *your natural way*, based only on how good we would have made each other feel in bed. I had to hurt your feelings and let you know that I no longer had desire for you simply because your body without any emotional intimacy between us, could have just as well belonged to any indifferent and impersonal woman.

In the morning you were late as if you didn't want to leave your room until I had finished cooking the Irish breakfast:
«Good morning beautiful.»
«Good morning beautiful he says!» you replied, namely:
"Why did you reject me if you think I am beautiful?"
You seemed in great emotional distress and avoided talking and even looking at me during the breakfast. Maybe you had cried before falling asleep the night before and you expected me to explain the reason for my cruelty. I had only defended my core beliefs for love, but in fact, I had crushed you and in doing so, I had shattered my own heart into pieces. I was very sorry for you, but it was much too late to talk about it, at that point nothing mattered anymore. Soon the silence became so deafening that I had to break it with some music.

Later on in the taxi to the airport:
«I left something for you in my bed.»
I looked at you and saw that you weren't wearing the necklace:
«I thought about it» you said.
Then at the airport you asked me a frequently asked question:
«Will you forget me within two months?»
«I will forget you as soon as you are out of my sight.»
I answered you as I had always done previously, but you still managed to keep your mask intact. We kept staring at each other for a while because I wanted to confirm a final farewell while you were hoping I would change my answer. Then before arriving to the boarding card control, you suddenly turned around and approaching me, you raised my glasses and came very close to my face, perhaps to check the color of my pupils or read me in the eyes and devastated me. In this very particular way, you practically made me understand in your own way that you had some feelings for me after all, and in doing so, you had definitely stabbed a dagger in my heart and wouldn't stop turning it around in the wound. This to me was an incontestable sign and made me wonder if you wanted me, but you had stubbornly refused to admit it until that moment. You had tried to tell me something very important in such a vague and lacerating way without really clarifying your feelings. A few moments later we arrived at the boarding card control where you approached me and opened your arms for a hug, but I spontaneously stopped you with a hand signal without thinking twice:
«Give me a hug.»
«I don't want to.»

Then I impulsively stretched out my arm as if to imply: *"Go now!"* and when you momentarily turned your head away in disbelief, I turned around and walked away without saying a word. I knew you were devastated because of the night before, but I couldn't imagine how you were feeling also after a cruel public breakup. You must have been completely destroyed.

I was letting go the woman that I still loved during the most dramatic and stressful event of my life and I wasn't coping. I did not hug you nor did I say goodbye because I was dying inside and I had to put an end to my suffering and to your efforts in an attempt to give me strong and essential reasons not to let you go. If we had hugged each other, you could have kissed my lips or worse, said an unexpected phrase that would have completely torn me apart. If that had happened, I couldn't have dealt with the situation, I wouldn't have been able to preserve my sanity and not only wouldn't I have let you leave, I would've never let you go. But your personality didn't convince me at all and most importantly, I didn't know anything about your motives. I was feeling so distressed that I had to run away from you before you tried to change my mind with another one of your last-minute stunts. I was trying to put as much distance between us as quickly as possible to alleviate the greatest trauma of my life without knowing what you really felt for me. I walked away from you in tears, remembering how I had run to Rubí with my heart in my hand. I left full of anger and deeply wounded, leaving you there shaken and embarrassed. I turned my back on you and making you feel unworthy of my love, I crushed your heart.

You were the only woman I had loved so ardently without even knowing you well, the only woman who had made me break down emotionally and cry over her. However, despite all my love and dedication, not only we had not touched each other's hearts and souls, we had even left deep emotional wounds in each other due to our insurmountable differences. After finding you, I had to let you down, hurt you and abandon you in a tormenting way for both of us. You had responded to my devoted feelings and noble intentions with nothing else but lies, manipulations, fictions and games. You had deceived me with all your facial masks, but you had never shown me your true face.

Personal growth

Returning home, I found three hundred euros in your bed; you had left them to cover some of my expenses. The gesture was nice, but I couldn't accept your money and I sent it back to you. My apartment felt utterly empty and I sensed an intense sorrow when I realized for the very first time in three years how lonely I was. I had purposely burned all the bridges behind me to make sure you would never contact me again, but about three hours after your departure, I received a message:

Hi Elias. I have just arrived home. Thanks for everything.

I couldn't understand why you had sent me a message after the way I had treated you. I was soon overwhelmed with guilt and wondered if I should take the first available flight to Barcelona, or if it was better to reply to you for now:

Isabel, I'm glad you arrived well and you're welcome.

I just couldn't stop thinking about you and for many nights I slept in your bed sheets until the scent of your skin on the pillow was washed away by my tears.

In early October, I went to Sweden while still thinking about why you had kept in touch. We had made a mess of everything, but I was still tormenting myself in a desperate quest to find out if you actually felt something for me. I don't know what happened, but when I saw you online, I got the urge to chat with you, but I really should have made a video call:

"Hi Isabel, how are you?"
"Hi Elias, I am fine. Are you in Stockholm?"
"Yes, as you know I had to renew my passport."
"How is Stockholm?"
"It's beautiful!
Isabel, do you know what day is today?"
"No, what day is it?"
"It's my birthday."
"Oh yes, I had forgotten. Happy birthday!"
"Thanks, I really wish you had accepted my previous invitation and had come to me to Stockholm.
...
Do you have any good news?"
"No, nothing."
"Have you returned to your ex?"
...
"No, not yet."
"Isabel, can I ask you a leading question?"
"Yes."
"How do you think you behaved during your stay in Ireland?"
"Good enough."
"Are you sure about that?"
"Yes."
I was going to ask if you had behaved in a similar manner also with the lawyer from Barcelona and you still couldn't understand why he had disappeared after only a month. But I refrained from sarcasm simply because you seemed to be completely oblivious about your behavior.

Strangely enough, you didn't say anything about the horrible way we had separated at Dublin Airport, nor did you mention anything about the events of our last night together as if nothing had happened. So I again decided to encourage you to a dialog: "I wonder if what I hoped for us would've been ideal considering that I am older than you."

...

"You were asking too much.

You expected from me what I couldn't give you."

I didn't expect such a comment. I hadn't actually done anything but waiting to find out your reason for coming to me. Besides, what you were insinuating wasn't exactly what had happened between us. I should have known you were denying the truth to satisfy your ego. I should have remembered your stubbornness which would have never allowed you to admit anything. I was right then; you wanted me only for sex and I had been too naive to believe that you had emotionally attached to me.

Then all of a sudden you wrote:

"You will never see me again."

"Oh really?"

"Yes."

"Why not?"

"Because we don't understand each other."

"Yes, you're right. Our problem is not just the language."

"Perhaps we can chat in another occasion."

"You don't even want to chat anymore?"

"No, I have to disconnect. Bye."

"I understand Isabel. Bye."

"You will never see me again?"
Fine, but why did you have to say it?
And why did you contact me after returning to Spain?
Wouldn't it have been better to leave everything as it was?
Maybe you couldn't accept the way we had separated and you wanted to be the one dumping me. Perhaps you wanted to keep in touch in case I would reconsider you, but after my comment, you had to give up right away. I should have thought about your behavior during your last days in Dublin. It seemed as if you did not want to lose me and had done everything except confiding in me, the only thing I cared about. Damn! I shouldn't have made that comment, there was still a chance.

I spent more sleepless nights in Stockholm and because I still couldn't make sense of anything, I decided to put an end to my frivolous and tormented desire for the truth. *"Lost love?"*
Reflecting on it felt like an obligation. But who had lost it?
At first, I thought I had lost the greatest love of my life, but then I had realized otherwise. Mine was just a physical loss, while the person who had really waisted a great opportunity to experience something extra ordinary was you, Isabel. I had realized that the loss was yours, while mine was a love that had only left me bitter in the mouth. By then I was so fed up with you that I cancelled our Facebook friendship and unlike your dear lawyer; I wrote all the facts and all my constructive criticisms about your behavior in a long email to awaken your self-awareness. It was the last nail in our coffin in the hope that you would realize why we really hadn't understood each other.

The next day I found your size for a brown autumn jacket from *H&M* that you hadn't found in Dublin city center and a beautiful black winter jacket you were previously looking for in Belfast. I also bought a box of the same chocolate that we had enjoyed together while we were traveling in Ireland and sent them all to you from Stockholm to show you that not only did I not hate you, I still cared a lot about you.

Meanwhile the infection had advanced again and was seriously threatening my life. After returning to Dublin, I consulted another private professor, Ryan O'Malley, and began a new treatment.
A few weeks later the professor declared to me:
«There have been no significant changes yet.»
«No? Well we have to keep looking for the right antibiotic.»
«Elias, your lungs are infected with a very rare and fast-growing mycobacterium.»
«Yes, I know, but there must be something else you can do.»
«I am sorry, there is nothing else I can do for you.»
«What are you saying?»
«I am saying I can no longer have you as my patient.
The mycobacterium has been resistant to all known antibiotics which have already been tested on you.»
«What am I supposed to do now?»
«I am truly sorry, I don't know.»
...
«How long do I have left?»
«Perhaps a year, but don't give up hope. I will present your case in our medical seminars in order to find you a cure.»

It was evident that all the treatments I had done up until then, had only slowed down the infection temporarily. Three years on, I was back at the starting point, except that my lungs were by now more damaged. I had to give up all hope and come to terms with this new reality. So I decided to come and see you one last time and as soon as possible before it was too late.

I had applied for a position as an aircraft maintenance engineer with Ryanair when one day I ended up in the emergency room at St. Vincent's University Hospital. While breathing oxygen, I got a call with the offer for the position that I wanted, but I had to decline. I was devastated, it felt as if my life was truly coming to an end. Then I noticed a team of three specialists from the department of respiratory medicine who had come to see me:
«Hi Elias, I am Professor James Murphy and these are Doctor Rosemary O'Brien and Doctor Liam Comely.
Professor O'Malley has told us about your unique case and now you are under our care. We will keep you in the hospital and try various antibiotics until we find the right one.»
I suddenly burst into tears without being able to speak, but I nodded as a sign of gratitude. They examined me and then made a few calls to find a bed for me. I was soon moved to a ward and then they started to test various antibiotics. In the meantime, all I could do was think about you. Your face was slowly fading in my mind and I couldn't access your profile because you must have blocked me. I was very disappointed and hoped I could at least dream of you, but apart from the occasional nightmares, I never had pleasant dreams.

It was very distressing to relive the unpleasant events that had occurred between us and comprehend why everything had gone so horribly wrong. If emotional pain is repressed, it could easily develop into harmful mental health problems. I knew none of us alone could ever overcome the pain and grief caused by our ordeal, unless we ourselves did something about it together. We both needed psychotherapy or it was only up to us to help each other. We needed to reconcile in order to understand what had happened and sort out our emotions, trying to relief each other's pain and heal our emotional wounds.

I recall how introverted you were because you felt rejected. You were resentful and threw angry glances at me to get my attention while hiding behind a thick stone wall. You practiced passive aggression to punish me for your pain and anger as a result of my lack of interest for you. An unfair and unjustified treatment that created insecurity and a very hostile atmosphere made up of awful feelings for both of us. A destructive behavior that could be regarded an emotional abuse aimed at control, but you had turned the situation around and considered yourself the victim. You didn't seem to be looking for love and spiritual connection as you didn't show the ability to feel or express emotions. You lacked empathic ability or emotional intelligence, so you weren't able to comprehend and appreciate your own feelings or those of others and create a relationship based on trust. You acted like an expert in pretending to be a strong and independent woman and blocked your beautiful and natural feminine weaknesses that made you a human.

Therefore, the need to present yourself so indifferent, was what prevented you from showing your vulnerability and experiencing emotions. As a result of pretending to be the woman you were not, you continued to have shallow relationships without ever being able to find love. Honesty is the most honorable quality that creates harmony between our thoughts, our feelings and our behaviors and showing vulnerability is the bravest way to express emotions, even when there is no reciprocity. I still liked the idea of you very much, but I wished you would first solve your emotional problems before looking for love.
Why stay in prison when the cell door is open?

In the meantime, I no longer bore the side effects of horrendous antibiotics or the depressive hospital environment. So one day I decided to escape, but I got lost in the maze of interconnected hospital buildings. Sometime later a security officer found me in delirium and crouched in a corridor between the departments and took me directly to the professor:
«What are you doing Elias?»
«I am not coping; I have to leave the hospital.»
«No, you can't leave now.
We are still trying to find a treatment for you.»
«I can't tolerate the side effects any longer.»
«Yes, we know that, but there is no other way.
If you leave now, you will die within a year.»
«I don't care, I am fed up» I told him while weeping.
«Listen Elias, you only need to take medication for some more months to survive this infection.»

«No!» I started to walk away and he followed me in the hall.
«Elias, wait! Listen to me, we are talking about your life. Please have more patience.»
I stopped and leaned against a wall, thinking.
«Stay with us a bit longer and we will send you home soon. What do you say?»
...
«I like the idea of returning home soon. Okay I will stay.»
They continued testing various antibiotics on me until eventually found a promising one. Then a surgeon inserted a thin plastic tube forty centimeters long through the main return artery in my right arm and directed it towards the entrance of the heart. After that, they sent me home where I received the antibiotic in saline solution by the home service through the tube in my artery for an hour, three times a day starting in early November.

I missed you a lot and that meant how much my life depended on you. I truly repented my conduct because I hadn't been the ideal version of myself. I had judged you fueled by unconscious prejudices and subjective opinions. But I didn't care anymore how you had behaved, except how wonderful you had made me feel. By then I knew you well enough to want to know who the real you were as you had briefly shown me. My empathy for you grew more each day and raised in me a sense of reverence for you. I saw you with an enlightened look and I no longer judged you because of your condition. If you were looking for love in the darkness of your circumstance, I should have acted like a bright beacon to guide you to me.

During the treatment at home, I had realized I hadn't understood your true state of mind. I had never had any previous experience with a woman suffering from depression and I lacked the know how to deal with you. Everything had become clear to me and I had realized that I had been blind, not realizing how desperately you had tried to attract my attention the only way you knew. You must have lost interest in the essential elements of a happy and solid relationship, maybe because you had been repeatedly hurt by men. You didn't appreciate my sincerity and total dedication because various factors prevented you from giving me a chance except for your willingness to have sex. My apprehension about you destabilized your need for belonging and this detachment added more pain and resentment to your inborn emotionality, making you scream silently under your mask.

I had realized that all we really needed was a little understanding or a few kind words to break down all your defenses and to clear all my doubts, but we had both failed. I had understood that what we had lacked was that first kiss or a tender touch to eliminate my frustration and to ease all your efforts in trying to reach me. But whatever wrongdoings we had committed, did not have to stay the same when we could have forgiven each other and changed our awful memories. Forgiving is very beneficial for mental health and reduces depressive states, anxiety and stress. Therefore I decided to stay in touch and encourage you to a reconciliation. I sent you many emails explaining my thoughts, my feelings and the reason for my behavior as well as repeatedly begging your forgiveness to make us both feel better.

I sent you Jennifer Lopez's *True Love* and later Eckhart Tolle's *The Power of Now,* both in Spanish in an attempt to help you conquer your depression. I also sent you beautiful Italian love poems to lift your spirit, happy birthday and season's greetings and made every effort to apologize to you for my wrong doings. I wanted you to vent your feelings and defend yourself against my accusations, but because you kept ignoring me, I decided to come and apologize to you in person.

However, my treatment would never end and eventually forced me to cancel my surprise visit to Rubí for that Christmas. So not only was I very depressed, but also trapped at home, trying to repress my despondency. I had to send you a message:

Beautiful Isabel

I had booked a room from December 21st to spend Christmas and New Year holidays in Rubí. I wanted to see you one last time to apologize, but I'm devastated because my treatment has ruined everything.

Your presents are already in my packed suitcase.

Greetings for the festive season

Elias

The next day I sent a few gifts to you and to your family that I knew only by name, but I couldn't send you one of your presents by air because it was liquid. One evening I was happily surprised when I accidentally found three photos of you in a duplicate file in the laptop. What a great joy it was to be able to see your face and your beautiful smile again. Staring at your photos made me feel closer to you and was the highlight of my daily life.

Soon my emotional intelligence had created an immense sense of empathy for you, and although empathy doesn't always mean love, love always involves a certain level of empathy. I realized I loved you with empathy for having done your best, but most importantly how adorable you could become. I could not wait to come and let you know, but Christmas was approaching fast and I was still stuck at home.

One day the nurse gave me the good news and told me the treatment would end in three days and then I would have to go to the hospital to remove the plastic tube in my arm. I had spent a month in hospital and by the end of the treatment, I would've spent more than three months in house arrest. I felt better than ever and I wanted to see you as soon as possible.
So I notified you with another message:

Dear Isabel

My treatment will end on February 12th, so I'm coming to see you in Rubí the next day to apologize to you.

I don't want to come knocking on your door unless you invite me or make an appointment to go out.

Let me know if you want anything from Dublin.

Elias

I flew to Barcelona February 13th, the day after my treatment ended. I sent you a message from Rubí and hoped you would want to see me, but I was wrong. The afternoon after Valentine's Day, when I saw your shutters in a different position, I rang your intercom and because there was no answer, I called you and left a message with a quivering voice.

Later on I sent you a message offering you a trip to Lisbon, where you had never been to give you another chance to vent your feelings, but all in vain. I was practically behind your door knocking and offering you the chance to forgive me as the best gift you could have given yourself. But it seemed as if you had been consumed by the desire to revenge and had decided to put into practice what you had told me during our last chat:
"You will never see me again."
I didn't understand how you could completely ignore me without at least appreciating the effort. You couldn't change the past, but you didn't know you could change the way you viewed it. Maybe you preferred to deny and forget your painful memories instead of reflecting on them and treasure the experiences. We could've seen each other even if you lived with a partner.

I was devastated and had to change my plans quickly. I didn't want to return home for a while, so I booked a flight to Lisbon and decided to leave your presents behind, but not even one entered your letterbox. I had to send you a package containing the perfume, *La vie est belle*, a box of Belgian chocolate and a white sheep plush from the post office just a few meters away from your building. However, shortly after in Lisbon I was still so traumatized that I decided to go to my family in Frankfort to distract my excruciating emotional distress caused by your refusal to see me.

The Friendship

I wanted to believe the infection had finally been eliminated and despite the failure in Spain, I was full of life again. I was with my sister Jazmin and her husband Filip who knew nothing about you. A Saturday morning when they had gone shopping, Jazmin called me and advised me that her friend Anna was coming to visit us. Anna was a forty-four-year-old German blonde that I had previously met at Jazmin's birthday party, but she knew nothing about my illness. A few minutes later the intercom rang, it was Anna. I opened the entrance and then the apartment door, waiting for her to walk up the last stairs to our level:

«Good morning Anna» I greeted her in English.

«Good morning Elias, how is it going?»

We kissed each other on the cheeks:

«Please come in. Nice to see you again.»

«What a pleasant surprise!

How long are you staying this time?»

«About two weeks. What are you up to?»

«Nothing special. I am busy working.»

«Great, and how is life? Are you still alone?»

«Yes, but I have many friends.»

«You are gorgeous.»

«Thanks!» she smiled flirtatiously.

We were both very excited to see each other again and none of us could stop smiling or taking our eyes off each other.

Then the intercom rang again: «Here they are!» I said.
I looked at Jazmin and Filip with a grin as I opened the apartment door for them and they smiled back at me. Anna stayed with us for one of her favorite meals prepared by my sister and we had so much fun that we decided to go out the next day.

She returned to us Sunday morning and then we walked all the way to Wacker's old and famous café and roastery in the city. Anna and I decided to sit outside in the sun, while Jazmin and Filip left us alone and sat inside:
«How about you Elias, do you have a girlfriend?»
«No, I have been lonely for a while.»
«Ah! How long has it been?»
I made a facial expression trying to remember how long it had been and started silently counting to my third finger. Next after a few moments of reflection, I kept counting quickly until I ran out of fingers. Then reacting extremely surprised, I looked at her in disbelief and using my index finger, I continued to point and count even with her fingers, making her laugh joyfully and grab and squeeze my hand in hers:
«Very recently, but I don't remember how long.»
Her smooth and velvety touch was so wonderful that we kept smiling and feeling each other's hands affectionately.
As we were talking, Anna received a couple of phone calls and I could see the name and the photo of a man on her display, but she kept declining them. Later we strolled in the city and after lunch at Kleinmarkthalle, we walked to Römerberg, the historic market square and then to an Irish pub.

On the way back, we took a shortcut and arriving in a nice park, we decided to rest for a while. Jazmin and Filip gave us some privacy again and sat a bit away from us:
«When can I see you, Elias?»
«I don't know. I have to return to Dublin next Thursday.»
«What do you say about this Tuesday?» she asked.
«Yes sure, call me.»
On Tuesday we met in the Irish pub in the city and hugged each other tightly. Anna ordered a mojito and I a Guinness:
Tell me Anna. Why have you never married?»
«Have you asked Jazmin about me?»
«Yes, I was curious to know why a beautiful woman like you has to live all alone.»
«Well, because it wouldn't make me happier. And you?»
«I have been married three times, although the first one was just a civil union.»
«Three times?» she said smiling.
«Yes, let's say I am not quite marriage material.»
«Do you have any children?»
«No, and I don't regret it!
But how come you don't have a boyfriend?»
«I have had many boyfriends.»
«So what happened?»
«Let's say I am on a break.»
I kept gazing into her blue eyes that reminded me of the ocean without blinking as I slowly approached her face and halted. Then she kissed me ardently, the way she wanted to be kissed. It was sweet and long enough to inhale her breath.

«Do you like Mediterranean cuisine?» I asked while retracting.
«Yes, very much.»
«Great! We have a reservation at *"Nummer 16".*»
«I don't know it.»
«It's a very popular Italian restaurant.»
«Let's go then, I have to buy a lipstick.»
«Don't worry, we still have time.»
After leaving the pub, she touched my hand and we held hands. We went to a department store and then she said:
«You go over there and look around.»
A few minutes later:
«Elias, come here. What do you think?»
She leaned slightly forward, rose her head a little, closed her eyes and formed her angelic lips into a sultry and sophisticated rosebud with a rare and stunning shade of burgundy.
I grabbed her face and kissed her tenderly:
«So you like the lipstick?»
«It makes you even more irresistible.»
«Okay, I will buy it» then she gently wiped my lips and left me relish the taste and the perfume of her lipstick.
We had fun in the restaurant and then we took a taxi to her place. We were both very cheerful and kept rubbing and squeezing each other's hands. Then as soon as we entered her apartment, I pushed her with my body against the door and grabbed her lower lip between my teeth. We started kissing as we undressed each other and moments later I carried her in my arms to the bedroom. In the morning we had breakfast in the neighborhood café and then she took the subway to work.

We met a few more times and for the weekend we went to see the Neuschwanstein Castle in Bavaria. We liked each other a lot, but Anna couldn't leave her mother alone in Germany and I couldn't live there because of the cold winters. We kept in touch for a while until we eventually drifted apart as time passed.

I could no longer afford a life in my beloved city Florence, so in April of that same year I relocated to Pianella, a nice village near Pescara. I bought an Alfa Romeo Giulietta in the name of an Italian friend because I wasn't officially a resident and rented a studio apartment in the countryside. Then I applied for the Italian residency and finally got it after about a month. I used to get very bored, so I started traveling without really enjoying myself. I missed you a lot and kept sending you postcards from various places with invitations to join me to travel around Italy, but you kept ignoring me. A few weeks later I developed a violent cough and as a consequence, hemoptysis. I attended the hospital and the doctor suspecting tuberculosis, isolated me in quarantine to make sure and in doing so, he left me all alone with my thoughts and passion for you again. One day I was so emotional that I decided to send you a message to let you know this was exactly how I had developed feelings for you during my illness in the course of the previous three years.

Hello Isabel

I hope you are well. I am quarantined in hospital for suspected tuberculosis, yet I don't feel all alone and completely abandoned because I still can feel your presence in my heart.

Elias

The coverage was weak, but moments later the phone beeped and I hoped with all my might that it was you:

Hi Elias

I hope you will recover and feel better soon.

Don't worry, just get well. I salute you

Isabel

Oh my God! I couldn't believe it and I had to double-check your name many times. How wonderful! You had answered me after months of absolute silence. But why?

Was it possible that I had finally reached you with my emails? Had you realized that you too had to take some responsibility for everything that had happened between us in Ireland?

I wanted to talk to you, but I had tears in my eyes and I'd have started to cry if I had called you. I wanted to believe that you had overcome all the unpleasant events in Ireland and had forgiven me. I hoped for your friendship and expected you to contact me again to make sure, but because you didn't, I thought you had replied to me only out of pity. Sometime later however, I just couldn't resist sending you another message thanking you and showing my appreciation for your kindness:

Dear Isabel

I hope I am not disturbing, especially if you live with a partner.

Thank you so much for your unexpected response.

It was a very pleasant and supportive surprise.

I want to believe you have forgiven me, so I feel very happy,

but on the other hand, I'm sorry for having lost you.

I wish you all the love and happiness.

Elias

Days later I decided to call you to find out how you were:
«Hi Isabel.»
«Hello Elias. How are you?»
«I feel much better these days.»
«Are you still in hospital?»
«No, it was a false alarm and they dismissed me after only a short week.»
«Very good.»
«How are you doing? Are you working?»
«No, but there is an official who is helping me to find work.»
«How is your financial situation?»
«I get unemployment benefits, but it has been reduced after the first two years.»
«How do you manage then?»
«Except for the mortgage I don't have many expenses.»
«I am not rich, but would you accept some money from me?»
«No, don't worry for me.»
«I am serious.»
«Thanks for the offer, but I can't.»
You talked too much about your unemployment and then:
«I have separated from my boyfriend for the second time.»
«I am very sorry, what happened?»
«Well, in addition to being bigoted and obtuse, he is also a couch potato and didn't want to go out with me.»
«What is his name?»
«Why do you want to know his name? For gossip?»
«No, I just want to know what to call him.
So, how is he doing without you?»

«He keeps saying: "You don't know how much you love me".»
«You haven't told him that?

...

Have you ever told it to anyone?

...

I on the other hand must admit that no woman has ever made me feel the way you still make me feel.»
«Thanks!»
«I would like to also sincerely apologize to you because what happened between us in Ireland was a real tragedy.»

...

«I have always considered you only a friend.»

...

«So Isabel, are you looking for a new relationship?»
«No, I don't know, relationships are very difficult.
I think I will have to take care of my brother Álvaro.»
«What? He is about my age, right?»
«Yes, but somebody has to take care of him when our mother leaves us.»
«What about your life?»
«I don't give a damn anymore.»
«That's not right. You really should think about your future.»
«I don't know, I don't know what is going to happen.»
«Yes, nobody can predict tomorrow, but you shouldn't give up.
Well Isabel, we have been talking for about an hour and my battery is running low.»
«Okay we should stop. Bye Elias.»
«Bye Isabel, stay in touch.»

So that's why you had replied to me. You had ended up alone again and maybe you were looking for a replacement for the ex. I thought you had fallen in love with him in a natural way, but obviously you couldn't live with him. Maybe he was your type just because he had the physical measurements and desirable proportions, but you hadn't evaluated the reasons that had led you to leave him the first time. Perhaps your choice of a partner was indeed indiscriminate and you preferred any validating or survival relationship in order to cope with yourself.

I didn't expect you to admit anything as far as I was concerned, but I was hoping you would agree we didn't have fun together. You seemed to deny yourself, declaring that you had always considered me only a friend. How could you so easily erase ten days and nights of your life full of events and intense emotions with a single lie? How could you undermine the reliability of my assessments and make me doubt reality? I don't know if you did it only to punish me or if it was an unconscious escape from reality to deceive yourself. I think you were in a state of denial, trying to fend off your suffering caused by the emotional pain. The denial process is another malicious defense mechanism, with which a person facing a bitter reality insists on rejecting it despite the irrefutable facts. Perhaps it brought you temporary relief, but you didn't know it was actually hurting you. Maybe your denial was also responsible for keeping you trapped in unhappy meaningless relationships and in such a difficult life situation, preventing you from recognizing your true reality and acting on your happiness.

The Spanish adventure

After about two years in Italy, I loaded my stuff in the Alfa and eventually arrived in Barcelona to embark on a new beginning in Spain, where the cost of living is lower. I drove to Rubí and saw that your apartment was as usual obscured. Then I went to browse in the entertainment center in your neighborhood, but I couldn't find you. Later on as I wandered and was about to turn a corner, I saw a woman who looked like you in the company of a younger man who could have been your ex. Looking at her for the time it took for us to pass each other, she saw me and smiled at me, maybe it was you recognizing me, but I still wasn't sure who she was and I didn't ascertain for obvious reasons.

I really wanted to see you a last time for a friendly closure, but I was afraid you would do anything to avoid me. Hence my joy and enthusiasm soon turned into emotional confusion. I spent hours thinking, trying to come to terms with my feelings against the facts. I had taken on your emotional problems and had put my heart and soul in trying to help you for more than two years, but all in vain. If in the end a mutual love had been born between us, there would still have been hope for us even after your return to Spain. I still cared for you and could have overlooked your negative qualities until you saw your own flaws as readily as you observed those of others. But I did not think you were serious and becoming a couple with me, was just a desperate attempt to involve me in another loveless and unhappy relationship until we would end it in bitterness.

Besides, you had repeatedly denied everything and had returned to your ex, causing a serious setback in making wise decisions in your best interests. Maybe you loved him or perhaps you had become so desperate that it was more important just to have a warm body to hug you, rather than thinking about how that body actually related to you. Perhaps the adverse effects of loneliness and the lack of physical intimacy eroded the self-esteem of a woman who could end up having an army of ex-boyfriends and lovers thanks to a live catalogue of men in the palm of her hand. However, continuing to count the stars, you may already have lost your moon forever.

By then I strongly believed you didn't have a complete emotional competence to recognize and respond to your own emotions or those of others, and despite a very innocent look, you had an unvirtuous nature. You pretended to be indifferent, but in reality, you adopted any ploy to achieve your purposes, hence you had triggered my self-protection instinct. Maybe you were unable of making serious commitment or didn't know how to love a man. Perhaps you started a relationship with anybody in order to maintain the bonds of dependence for your childhood desires and fantasies. But because you kept refusing to recognize and acknowledge your own flaws, whenever you felt compelled to react to criticism, you panicked and continued to play games, to pretend and to manipulate. Then when these bonds eventually broke and you ended up alone again, you considered yourself the victim and blamed only the partner without taking your share of responsibility and in the end, you turned to vengeance.

You showed a false sense of strength, but behind this mask of overconfidence, you had a low self-esteem and a constant need to be loved. You did not like being judged negatively, nor did you appreciate constructive criticism. The fact is you had asked me for advice, which didn't mean I was wiser than you, but that I had recognized a harmful behavior. I cared about your best interests and had the courage to tell you what you needed to know. Having also taking on all the blames, I had asked for your forgiveness for more than two years, but unsuccessful. I didn't want to be one of your sexual partners or your last choice. I had resisted all your manipulations trying to make you change your ways. I had actually offered you the most natural therapy without being aware of it at the time, but you hadn't been able to break out of your ego's prison. If you didn't want to change your life by changing your ways for your own good, you wouldn't ever have a future with anyone. I realized it no longer made sense trying to influence you in order to help you the way I had done until then. I had to find a simple but more effective approach to reach you passively, but I still didn't know how?

The next day I crossed all of Spain to Portugal and arrived in my favorite village Sintra near Lisbon where I considered staying, but then I decided to go to Tavira in Algarve. However, a week later I returned to Spain because Spanish is more like Italian and traveled all over Andalusia in search of a nice place. Later on I backtracked and returned to the beautiful village of Grazalema in south west of Spain where I finally decided to settle down and soon after I rented a two-story house.

One day I received a message in English on *Messenger*:

Good evening Elias

Please don't disturb my girlfriend Isabel any more.

Your behavior is not normal, especially at your age.

Juan Carlos

I never thought I was disturbing or stalking you and I couldn't understand why you had involved me in your relationship or why I had a message from your ex, unless you had returned to him for the second time. In any case, I sent you the receipt of the necklace which for me was a painful memory and I promised not to contact you ever again.

I settled in Grazalema and began studying Spanish with the books you had given me. I also started traveling, but I used to get sad because I missed you by my side. One day the village librarian told me about her former workplace where there would have been an opportunity for me. She told me I could use my knowledge of English and teach the children in Ronda. Later on I met the director of the academy who asked me to attend the classes of other teachers to learn how to teach. The academy had mostly local teachers, but also two English girls, one Scott and one American lady. I attended their classes, observing their methods that didn't always seem correct to me. I met everyone, including Linda, a married Spanish woman who I couldn't bear to hear. She had a very strange voice and shouted during her lessons in order to be heard by the much younger children who constantly screamed. Soon after I started my own lessons and considering my lack of experience, I was doing very well.

One Saturday my French friend Élise and I drove to the lake side village of Zahara, another one of those *"White villages"* in the region and then went to a restaurant. After lunch, I noticed Linda approaching our table to pick up the bill.
We were both surprised to see each other:
«Linda? What are you doing here?»
«I work here, it's our restaurant.»
«Wow! I had no idea.»
«Did you like the food?»
«Yes, my steak was cooked just the way I like it.»
«And my salmon was delicious» Élise said.
«Thanks a lot. Here is the bill.»
I was just about to hand over the money:
«Oh look Linda. You have cut your finger.»
«Ah yeah, it looks like it.»
The small cut was where her wedding ring would have been:
«Let me take care of it» I said.
I wiped her finger with a clean tissue. Then I grabbed the hand sanitizer from my bag to sterilize the wound, after that I covered it with a plaster and both ladies found my meticulous care, cool. Linda thanked me and then we left.

We teachers often discussed our low salaries and the unpaid hours for lesson preparations and exam corrections and I always used to cross my arms. After a while Linda started putting her hand on my bare arm any time a few of us were talking about our work conditions, but because I didn't like her, it didn't mean anything to me.

I knew many people touch their friends to show their trust for them, but Linda kept holding my arm until we finished talking, making her appear very affectionate. Colin, the Scottish teacher used to tease me saying that Linda wanted to have fun with me for a while, but he didn't know I have always avoided an affair with a married woman.

Despite having an income in Spain, I missed Italy and everything Italian. I used to follow Italian tv series on the Spanish television and every time I watched *Chief Inspector Montalbano* in original language, I wondered what I was doing in Spain. Meanwhile, Linda had started to wear elegant clothing and her voice was even becoming sweet to my ears. One morning during the break I saw her looking at me through the window and seemed very upset, so I immediately went to her classroom:
«What is the matter Linda?»
«I am going through a tough time recently.»
«Why? What's wrong?»
«I am in the process of divorcing my husband.»
«Oh my God! What happened?»
«For what he has done, I have to divorce him.»
«I am very sorry, come here» we hugged.
«I admire your courage. Hang in there.»
«And how are you Elias?»
«As you already know, I am not happy with this job.»
«Well, you should stop doing it.»
«Yes, I think I should.»
Then I left when I saw the children returning to their classes.

A few days later I was in the office to meet Christine, the new British teacher when Linda also joined us.

We greeted each other and then the secretary asked her:

«Do you know Elias is leaving?»

«Yes, he has told me.»

Then she approached me and put her hand on my arm again:

«When will you resign?»

«As soon as Christine can take over my classes.»

I don't remember what else we said as her touch aroused such wonderful sensations in me that my mind was absent. Perhaps she was showing affection and had triggered chemical reactions in me. She had actually provoked a vague tone in me, which is the activity of the vague nerve, a branch of the subconscious and autonomous nervous system. Linda stimulated my pressure receptors every time she put and held her hand on my arm and eventually had made me want to bond with her. Then as she was walking out, she withdrew her fingers very slowly from my arm until the distance between us was about to completely cut our contact. I couldn't resist her anymore, so uncrossing my arms, I grabbed her hand and approached her smiling in the hall:

«Do you work in the restaurant this Saturday night?»

«Yes, like every week end.»

«I will come for dinner.»

«Okay! See you later.»

I didn't want to flatter myself and speculate about why Linda liked to touch me and even though I wanted to have a family, for obvious reasons I could not get involved with a forty-year-old woman and her two young children.

Saturday night I went to their restaurant and enjoyed watching Linda as she served me. Later on I walked to catch up with her in an isolated area at the rear of the restaurant:
«How is it going Linda? You must be tired.»
«No, we weren't busy. Did you like the food?»
«Yes thanks. It was good with generous portions.»
«Then you should take me to the Gran Canarias.»
«What? Are you serious?»
«Yes, I like the Canaries very much.»
«How is the divorce going?»
«I have to wait until it's granted.»
Then there was an alluring silence during which I could see the curiosity in her eyes and the lines of joy around them as my eyes studied her face. Next I began swinging my gaze between her bright eyes and her full lips which made me lose a heartbeat. I grabbed her arms and pulling her to me, made her suddenly part her lips gasping for air. Her perfume smelled like jasmine and her warm breath was enticing. I kissed her gently, relishing her soft and luscious lips as she was kissing me back.
Then we smiled at each other and moments later I left.

She called me late Sunday morning:
«Good morning Elias, what are you up to?»
«Hi Linda. I am studying Spanish.»
«Would you like to go for a coffee in about an hour?»
«Yes, it would be a pleasure.»
«Can you pick me up at the entrance to the Moorish ruins?»
«Yes of course.»

About an hour later I picked her up and decided to take her to one of my favorite cafés in Villaluenga:
«What happened between you and your husband?»
«I don't want to talk about it.»
«Okay!»
«Are you looking to buy a house?» she asked me.
«Oh no, I can't buy anything anymore.»
«What do you mean?»
I told her about my chronic illness and why I was in Spain.
«Ah, I am very sorry. Anyway, we have a nice house in Zahara that you could rent if you want.»
«No thanks. I have to return to Italy soon.»
«Aren't you happy here?»
«No, I haven't been happy lately no matter where I go.»
«Why? Because of your illness?»
«Yes, but also because I don't like to live alone.»
...
On the way back when my music was playing *Broken vow* by Lara Fabian, I noticed she had gone very quiet.
Moments later she suddenly burst into tears:
«What happened?»
«It's this song.»
«Oh my God, no!»
«Yes, he betrayed me.»
«I am so sorry.»
I stopped the music and pulled over on the side of the country road to pay all my attention to her:
«It must have been devastating. How did you find out?»

«One day as I went to join him on the balcony, I saw him writing *"I love you"* in a message to somebody and when I asked who he loved, he finally confessed.»
«Vaya! Did you know his lover?»
«Yes, Teresa, the butcher's wife and to humiliate us further, later on they began to go out together hand in hand.»
«Damn! Come here» we hugged.
«Don't think about it anymore. You have made the right decision and everything is going to be all right» then I wiped her tears.

During the next week we met every day at the academy, but we didn't talk about us. On Friday evening there was a small party in my honor in the neighborhood café, but Linda was absent. I asked the director who told me she was the only one having a lesson. I called her on Saturday morning and in the afternoon, we went to *Venta La Vega*, a nice rural family run café, restaurant and hostel on the way to Ronda:
«Tell me Elias, have you ever had a heartache?»
«Yes of course! It has been an inevitable part of my life.»
«What has happened to you?»
She was attentively listening to me as I briefly told her my story with you Isabel:
«It's very upsetting. Do you still think about her?»
«Yes, I still think she needs help.»
«Wow! That's love, true love.»
«True love! What else should love be but only true.»
«What are you going to do now?»
«I have to conclude my life here and prepare to leave.»

«When do you have to return to Italy?»
«If I am not going to apply for residency in Spain, I have to do the car inspection in Italy by the end of July.»
«Ah, you still have more than two months to go.
Why don't you stay in Spain for as long as possible?»
«I would like to, but it wouldn't be a good idea.»
«Why not?»
«Because I might get attached to you.»
«Vaya! Are you falling in love with me?» she asked joyfully.
«Well, let's say you are growing on me.»
«What do you like about me?»
«You are gorgeous, you know what you want and how to get it.
I have never admired a woman as much as I admire you.»
«And what do you think I want?»
«Everything that I still long for.»
She reacted as if I had hit a soft spot.

I moved out of my home at the end of the month and moved to *Venta La Vega*. I advised her and she came to see me the next day. I had a studio on the ground floor in front of the pool in a small rose garden with a few sheep and an ostrich wandering on the other side of the fence. When Linda came:
«Oh what a beautiful place, I had heard about it.
How long are you going to stay here?»
«I don't know, I think I should leave soon.»
«Why in such hurry?»
«Because I don't want to complicate things.»
...

Considering Linda's best interests, I had no honorable reason to stay just to take advantage of a hurt woman. Saturday night I went to their restaurant. She was talking to somebody, but when she saw me, she knew why I was there. I ordered a beer at the counter, looking at her and listening to her voice which by now meant a lot to me. When she came to me:
«Elias, what a surprise! Have you come to dine?»
«No, I have come to say good bye.»
«What? Why do you have to leave so soon?»
I took a deep breath as I looked at her with a smile:
«Thanks a lot for making me feel so alive, but as much as I like to, I don't want to end up falling in love with you.»
I wished her all the best and got up to leave. She didn't know how to handle the situation and when she attempted to hug me, I held out my hand instead. I kissed her hand and smiling at her, I walked away. When I reached the door and turned around for one last look, I saw her looking at me, stunned.
I smiled at her again and after a bow, I left.

I had to drive to Barcelona to reach Italy, so I decided to pass through Rubí to see discreetly how you were doing. I arrived at your building around ten pm and saw that you were still closing the curtains and lowering the shutters almost completely. I didn't think you did it for safety on the third floor of a secure building. It was a clear indication of the state of your mind and I couldn't believe you could still be suffering. Such a depressive routine meant that you were still dealing with severe negative feelings about yourself and the need to hide.

You must have suffered many heartaches because of your failed relationships, but I doubt you ever had a similar trauma to what we went through together. I must have caused you more agony and even though it had already been a long time, it seemed as if you still hadn't recovered from your experiences. You couldn't have been able to do it, unless you had understood your true state of mind, recognizing that you are suffering from something more sinister than depression and decided to deal with it rather than just consuming pills. But referring to your lack of reaction to my reconciliation efforts, your history and the way you still needed to hide, it didn't seem likely at all.

The next day I would have crossed the Mediterranean from Barcelona to Civitavecchia near Rome, but I decided instead to take the highway and reach Italy via southern France. I had lived in remorse for too long and despite the uncertainty about your real situation, I was very worried about you. I still wanted to help you and prevent my pain from becoming the greatest regret of my life. When I arrived in Italy, I continued to drive without being able to find a place I could afford. Then from Gangi in Sicily I returned to the mainland Italy and headed towards Puglia again. In Brindisi I drove to the port and as soon as I realized a ferry was about to leave for Igoumenitsa, I got on board with the urge to go on. In Greece I continued until Sofia and after visiting the city, I left Bulgaria. A few days later I ended up in Izmir where I decided to return to Istanbul. I was considering to live in Turkey where the cost of living is very low, but later on I returned to Italy and eventually found a nice home by chance in Calabria.

In these three weeks of pilgrimage through six countries, I had traveled about twenty thousand kilometers, during which I had finally forgiven myself. I had also thought about finding a way to create a curiosity for you and thus influence your mind. I had to describe the events in great details and reason with you in order to awaken your awareness about your mental state. So I decided to do some research and analyze your behavior and came to believe that you suffer from an extreme emotional distress. But I knew I could no longer talk to you and I couldn't do it with multiple emails or a long letter that you could discard without reading. From there, the idea was born to review *Lost love* and to elaborate it to obtain this novel, no matter the level of my Italian, my writing style or how long it would take.

The hypothesis

You believed to be suffering from depression because of too many heartaches and maybe you have turned to your doctor without revealing anything about your ways with others and your feelings about yourself. But if these failures have caused you an emotional impediment that continues to deepen, antidepressant can't change the way you think. Besides, they would numb your senses and add many nasty side effects including any complex combination of the more serious ones:

- increased nervousness
- drowsiness and fatigue
- post-traumatic stress disorder
- obsessive compulsive disorder
- neuropathy, pain from damaged nerves
- generalized anxiety and social anxiety disorders
- bipolar disorder or severe depression with fluctuating moods and intense changes in thinking and behavior

Antidepressants are pharmacologically inert substances with no therapeutic function. They have a placebo effect and have been designed only to appease depressed people and are prescribed by arrogant doctors who neglect all other forms of non-drug treatment. Hence becoming addicted to pills unrelated to many factors that cause depression and with serious side effects, is obviously very wrong and must be avoided.

No, I am not a psychologist, but I spent enough time with you to see and verify the tale tell signs of a very wrong image that you have of yourself. We all have an inferiority complex to some degree, but in your case, it may have become a problem thanks to your failed relationships. As a result of your silent suffering and the lack of recognition by others, you pity yourself and have to find a way to feel good, but because of the insecurities, you can't fulfil this desire and the repeated failures have caused you more pain and anger. Hence, you have been forced to resource to damaging behavior towards others to make them feel inferior and this way become superior. But every time your natural need for a partner fails, you isolate yourself and this further aggravates your sense of unworthiness and pushes you even deeper in depression. This reaction is actually a cry for help, but it is often very difficult to hear and respond to these silent cries. You were the first victim of your condition and you have never intuited the wounds you leave on those who have been emotionally involved with you. Whoever gets to know you, has to save himself rather than help you end your vicious circle.

An expert can distinguish between a depression, an emotional distress due to painful interpersonal relationships or a possible mental disorder caused by various difficulties in daily life since childhood. But because you do not think there is anything wrong with you, even if you agree to see a psychologist, you would not be able to describe your ways or behave as you did with me, so it would not be possible to make a psychiatric assessment due to the lack of so many important elements.

I would have assumed as the only daughter after three brothers, you would have been spoiled developing a superiority complex, but your characteristics don't fit a narcissist person. Maybe the behavioural inhibition practiced by your parents forced you to repress all your emotions and adopt negative feelings for your natural weaknesses. Perhaps this prohibition suffered during the sensitive stages of emotional development in your childhood, prevented you the formation of self-regulation. It is the ability to identify, modulate and express one's inner states and it is vital for structures of interpersonal attachments, awareness of one's actions, the sense of self and the ability to communicate. Those unaware of suffering from *"Emotional dysregulation",* that is to say; the improper canalization of emotions, could be emotionally very unstable and even show extreme variations of emotionality. Such people could feel chronically dejected and disconnecting themselves from the reality of their own experiences, choose to isolate themselves and have to constantly regulate their feelings externally with antidepressants.

But I can also think of an adorable young woman longing for love and happiness who has been repeatedly hurt by those she loved. As a result, you may still be wondering why things have always gone so wrong and because you can't find the answers, you have developed feelings of worthlessness. You must have been intimately hurt and this has changed your attitude towards what you want the most, love. So even when a nice man comes along, you become rational with your prejudices which basically leads both of you to another heart-breaking end.

The succession of negative thoughts or mental rumination is a dead-end circuit that strengthens your negative condition. Your thoughts are not who you are, you need to step out of your comfort zone and reframe them to find a natural solution to your emotional problems. You should do some research in order to get to know yourself and questioning your negative thoughts and feelings, change the misperceptions of yourself and the unpleasant past events. If you just could change your way of thinking and rely on your feelings, everything will change and you will be able to put an end to all this negative energy that has been holding you back. But you shouldn't pretend, transform yourself and be who you really want to be, starting with:

- Leave all the past behind.
- Stop taking antidepressant pills.
- Belittle the time spent on social media.
- Engage in a weekly outdoor physical activity.
- Spend more time with the family and go out with friends.
- Choose a healthier diet and wake up early in the morning.
- Make the right move leaving behind all the terrible memories and relocate near the sea, where you have always wanted to live.
- If you are still unemployed, go around looking for any work or volunteer in order to feel useful and involved in the community.
- Smile at life, make new friends, get out in nature, read books, improve your Italian, learn the Latin dances, go travelling, etc.

Healthy habits will change the view of yourself and will give you self-confidence. When you feel good and can respect yourself, you will become sincere and will have empathy and compassion which in turn will teach you to love and to forgive.

These measures will improve your overall well-being, however to avoid repeating patterns of negative thoughts and feelings, it is also necessary to eliminate all sources of negativity in your life, including *dear* people. Your heart is not just a pump, it's the center of your emotions and the essence of your spiritual being. You should integrate the logic of your head with the whispers from your heart. That is to say, you must start listening to your heart, because the guidance it gives you is in your best interest and is based on your natural instincts and intuitive intelligence. When you experience gratifying changes that relieve your pain and make you feel happy with yourself; you will appreciate them and will definitely want to continue on this path.

You may already know your problem, but you may still be going through various stages of denial and confusion for resistance to change before reaching acceptance. If you by now are aware of it and have accepted it, you are halfway to practice self-help and can reap great benefits in transforming your life. If not, you must first have that inner dialogue with yourself and attempt to get to know your psyche. Then you should seriously engage in self-help, trying to resolve your emotional problems on your own, because the only person who can really help you, is you. What a great confidence boost it would be, if you could manage to free yourself from negative thoughts and feelings on your own and without relying on a psychologist to indoctrinate you and get you addicted to pills. Non-drug self-help is very satisfying and could become your best advisor and will always be available whenever you need it.

With an effective self-therapy, you should soon be able to lead a life of dignity where sincerity with yourself and everyone else, will directly reflect on your inner peace and emotional harmony. One day when you finally manage to identify your ideal self, you will feel free and you will want to demolish the stone wall that has held you prisoner and you will be able to fall in love for real. I'm sure everything else will fall into place in due course. None of this will happen overnight, however, with your commitment, perseverance and emotional support from your family and true friends, it will all happen in stages.

My inspirations for you

This story is our legacy and it's dedicated to you to arouse your hidden inner wonder and to make you understand where the serenity of a better life might come from. It is intended to cause a deepening of your mental state in a rational way, so that you become aware of the root of your emotional problems without activating your defence mechanism of denial. Reflecting on our history is like looking in the mirror or listening to your inner voice. I believe it can encourage you to travel in your mind and make you discover your true values which will help you become who you really want to be.

I hope you will find me and let me know if this story one day causes a ripple effect in your mind and everything eventually becomes clear in your eyes. You will understand that you don't need to go far to find the love you deserve because this emotion initially arises from loving and respecting yourself. Then you will want to shamelessly remain vulnerable, because you will know that your vulnerability is a vigorous driving force for connection and the only source and reason for your beautiful and natural needs for emotional intimacy and love.

Someday you will be able to follow your heart with pride, to want to express your feelings and affection with words and use your natural intuition resolutely to fall in love for the right reasons. It will happen when you unlock your lonely heart and finally allow love to overwhelm it with your inborn emotionality, perhaps for the very first time. Only then, will you realize that you should have never been afraid of love, on the contrary, you should have fallen in love a long time ago to let yourself be lulled by the power of love. Only then, will you feel reborn and be able to shine and be all the woman you truly are. Maybe then you could finally feel my love for you and realize that no one has ever loved you as much as I do. Perhaps you would also appreciate that the most excruciating part for me wasn't having to let you go, but still liking the idea of you for love.

Lost on the high seas

Like a true nomad, I walked many paths,
I lived my days near and far, low on plains, high on plateaus.
serenity I desired, happiness I pursued,
love I sought.
I found nothing but disappointment,
I was a lost ship on the ocean among the waves,
never reaching the shore.
Suffering for love and feeling blue,
the promise was made, my heart I will give no more,
until our routes met for an instant
and your dance was captured in me.
In my desolate soul, hope kindled a flame,
a seed sprouted in my forsaken heart,
with the wind in my sails, I will follow you towards the sun
and let destiny lead us wherever it wants.
Loneliness no longer exists, immersed in me are you,
the abundance of your affection, living in my heart,
brings me passion with an immense vigour.
Tender is your love, sheltering my vitality without fear,
dissipating all my pain,
dazzled by your beauty and your sweet spirit,
I still want you for love.

Printed in Great Britain
by Amazon

64250595R00090